~

*THE
AGE OF
MACKINTOSH*

~

ARCHITECTURAL

The Journal of the Architectural Heritage Society of Scotland

HERITAGE III

~

THE
AGE OF
MACKINTOSH

~

EDINBURGH

University Press

1992

The Architectural Heritage Society of Scotland

Glasite Meeting House
33 Barony Street
Edinburgh EH6 6WX
Tel: (031) 557 0019

AHSS Publications Sub-Committee:

Nic Allen, MA, DipTP (*Chairman*); Ian Gow, MA; Shelagh Kennedy, BA (*Newsletter Editor*); John Lowrey, MA (*Journal Editor*); Gillian Haggart, MA (*Book Reviews Editor, from 1991*); Elizabeth Strong, BA (*Book Reviews Editor, to 1991*).

Editorial Advisory Board:

William Brogden, BArch, PhD, FSAScot; Jane Durham; John Frew, MA, DPhil; Ian Gow, MA; James Macaulay, MA, PhD, FRHistSoc; Charles McKean, BA, FRSA; David Walker, DA, FSAScot, FRIAS (Hon), LID (Hon).

This publication has been generously sponsored by a grant from the Scottish International Education Trust, to whom the Society wishes to express its gratitude.

Manuscripts for submission to *Architectural Heritage* should be sent to John Lowrey, c/o the Architectural Heritage Society of Scotland, as above.

Architectural Heritage III is the nineteenth issue of *The Journal of the Architectural Heritage Society of Scotland* (formerly the *Scottish Georgian Society*). Backnumbers (1, 7–11, 13, 15) are available from the Society. *Architectural Heritage I: William Adam* (1990) and *Architectural Heritage II: Scottish Architects Abroad* (1991) are available directly from Edinburgh University Press.

Membership of the Society entitles members to receive both *Architectural Heritage* and the regular *Newsletters* free of charge. The Society exists to promote the protection and study of Scotland's historic architecture. Details of membership can be obtained from the Society's headquarters.

Transferred to Digital Print 2010

Edinburgh University Press
22 George Square, Edinburgh ι

Typeset in Lasercomp Perpetuι
by Alden Multimedia Ltd.

Printed and bound in Great Britain by
CPI Antony Rowe, Chippenham and
Eastbourne

A CIP record for this book
is available from the
British Library

ISBN 0 7486 0382 4 (limp)

CONTENTS

Introduction

THIS ISSUE of the *Journal of the Architectural Heritage Society of Scotland* takes as its starting point a conference, organised by the Strathclyde group of the Society as part of Glasgow's 1990 celebrations, on 'Mackintosh's Successful Contemporaries'. Some of the papers from that conference, with changes and additional material, make up the contents of the present volume.

In 1983, the Charles Rennie Mackintosh Society held a conference under the title *Charles Rennie Mackintosh: National and International*.[1] The main purposes of the conference were to look at Mackintosh's interest in traditional forms of Scottish architecture as means of freeing architecture from the accepted styles of the time and to consider the possible influence of his work on the European and American avant-garde. The emphasis was very much on Mackintosh's international reputation, and the Scottish context of his work did not figure prominently in the discussions.[2]

Was it really the case that Mackintosh was the single, lonely genius whose work far outshone that of his 'second-rate' compatriots, or have the merits of other Scottish architects been unfairly eclipsed by the huge reputation of Mackintosh? One problem here is that very little is known about many of Mackintosh's contemporaries, and it is the purpose of this book to introduce a number of the most interesting architects and to assess their achievements. In one case, that of John James Burnet, the relationship with Mackintosh, in terms of career, possible influence, public perceptions and in personal terms, is looked at in some detail and with surprising results.

In general terms, perhaps the most striking feature of the work discussed here is its enormous breadth and variety of styles, from the Beaux-Arts classicism of Burnet to the polychromatic Venetian Gothic of Leiper or the French Renaissance of Browne. As Mike Davis and Deborah Mays show, there was tremendous interest in English styles, while at the same time Scottish architecture was studied and adapted for modern needs by Mackintosh himself. A different aspect of this interest in Scottish work is discussed in Harriet Richardson's chapter on Lorimer's castle restorations; though even here the emphasis was on adaptation for modern needs.

In Gavin Stamp's chapter, he emphasises that it was Mackintosh's perceived freedom from historicist styles which was partly responsible for his elevation as a 'pioneer of modern design'.[3] Conversely, the careers of many of his contemporaries have been ignored until fairly recent years precisely because they were seen as the products of Victorian and Edwardian eclecticism and historicism.

Whatever the level of their achievements, one thing is clear. It is to architects like the ones discussed in this book that we must look to gain a clear picture of the development of our great cities in the late nineteenth and early twentieth centuries. In Glasgow, Mackintosh's contemporaries transformed the city, both by expanding its suburbs and by rebuilding its centre. Since most of the architects discussed in this volume were Glasgow-based or had Glasgow connections, it is fitting to look, very briefly, at the world in which they lived and worked and to show the broad effect of their output on the cityscape.

Glasgow at the end of the nineteenth century was a city teeming with energy, and, despite the impressive building programme of the previous fifty years, it was a city still impatient to get ahead, to expand yet further, and where necessary to start rebuilding over the work of preceding generations.

The Glasgow Subway was opened during these years, and contemporary photographs show in graphic detail how whole streets were ruthlessly ploughed up for the lines, with the inevitable casualties among existing buildings as a result. It was during these years also that the horse-drawn tram network, having been taken under municipal control, was expanded and converted to electric traction. Both these developments in transport brought new areas on the periphery of Glasgow into easy contact with those places of work within the city and allowed the more mobile middle and upper working classes to move out.

The city centre, by comparison, was losing its indigenous population with the displacement of many thousands of poor, mostly of Irish immigrant stock, out of the High Street and surroundings, as the demolitions ordered by the City Improvement Trust took their toll. And when Glasgow began seriously to rebuild itself, it did so in a different *colour*. No longer were the cream and grey sandstones of the nearby Giffnock or Kenmure quarries called for, but the fresh discoveries of Lochabriggs, Dumfries and Ballochmyle *red* sandstones were rushed in by the still expanding railway companies.

It was a period when major civic buildings were being built, such as the City Chambers (William Young 1888) or the galleries at Kelvingrove (J.B. Simpson and E.J. Milner Allen 1901), all symbolising in stone that Glasgow was a major, confident and cosmopolitan city. The *Builders Journal* of 1906 devoted an entire issue to 'New Buildings in Glasgow', an accolade hitherto only accorded to Liverpool (outside London). Because of the sheer number of new buildings in the city over recent years, the article was forced to restrain itself to looking at the achievements of only the previous four years—although this was stretched a little to include the first phase of the School of Art.

Glasgow had survived one of the greatest financial crashes in Western Europe only a few years earlier in the City of Glasgow Bank Crash of 1878, and had proved itself capable of not just stepping but positively *leaping* out of the shadow which had threatened to engulf it. As if to prove this, it staged three major International Exhibitions—the 1888 with its strong Oriental theme, the 1901 which illustrated the leaps and bounds taken in the fields of science, industry and art and with the buildings taking on a Spanish Baroque idiom, and the 1911, with a similar theme but on a smaller scale and with a stronger Scottish flavour to the architecture.

It was a time when the Arts in their widest sense came to the fore and began to form part of the everyday life of much of the population—which in reality meant the growing ranks of the middle classes. As Juliet Kinchin has described in her essay on 'The Glasgow Girls',[5] it was a time when men encountered 'art' in their daily world of manufacture and business, when buying fine art for exhibitions or as mere investment in a commodity. Women, on the other hand, were the consumers of art—visiting exhibitions, choosing household fabrics or even taking tea and muffins in one of Miss Cranston's Tea Rooms.

Sculpture on buildings became more figurative, yet more symbolic and potent than ever before, while intense and vivid stained glass seemed equally at home occupying municipal chambers in the city centre and WC windows in Hyndland. The buildings themselves became more riotous, more unfettered and more fluid both in their architectural composition and in the physical circulation they permitted.

More flexible building regulation recognising the technological advances made during these years appeared. New methods of construction were used, such as the reinforced concrete used by James Salmon II and J. Gaff Gillespie in Lion Chambers (1905), the steel frame used by John A. Campbell in the Northern Assurance Building of 1909 (perhaps expressed more obviously in the wide spacing of the glazing behind), and the lift. All these allowed architects to design higher buildings (up to 100 feet) with greater floor areas, uncluttered by thick, load-bearing walls, which meant that the relatively small plot ratios which the existing Georgian or early Victorian buildings occupied could be profitably redeveloped without expensive and time-consuming accumulation of neighbouring sites.

For all the preceding reasons of technological advancement, the spread of the 'artistic' and mass outward-looking exhibitions, it was clear that Glasgow was on the verge of profound change. No longer was it merely satisfied with the beautiful conformity and regularity of the early nineteenth-century classical tradition where a status quo of mutual consent and technological constraint conspired to keep buildings relatively low and, by and large, not seeking too much attention for themselves.

During this period, the airspace over Glasgow was up for sale and Glasgow began to develop a skyline, and it was a skyline of more than just church spires. Banks, legal chambers, offices and warehouses—basically anything that could afford a lift—reached for the skies and capitalised on their expensive city sites. Building was mostly speculative, and this was reflected both in the shaking-off of a 'house style' and in a showy clamour for a perhaps less dignifying attention in the use of turrets, corner domes and tall chimney stacks set amid steep mansards and spiky dormers.

The confidence of this great, mainly red, sea of building that it was heralding a new, unstoppable tide must have been absolute, because, for all the polished adornment of main elevations, sides were often left as rough-finished brick gables, each obviously awaiting the spurt upward of its 'inevitable' neighbour to clothe its nakedness. Perhaps, however, we should be grateful that the wholesale rebuilding of entire city blocks did not occur. In a curious way, Glasgow's streetscape actually works with these sometimes huge discrepancies of scale, resonant of a period in which both citizens and architecture just could not be 'kept down'–aspirations were just too big and municipal or perhaps corporate pride all-pervasive.

The other notable mark made on the city was that of new housing. In the field of tenement-building, stricter Public Health Acts, and in particular the Burgh Police Scotland Act of 1892, began to enforce changes, such as the limiting of the number of flats in each common stair and the compulsory provision of running water and WCs in dwellings. Built-in wooden box-beds were to be phased out, although plans continued to feature the area given over to the bed recess for many years to come.

One of the main movers in the provision of new, particularly working-class housing in Glasgow was the City Improvement Trust, and this body made full use of the architects available in the city, with some stunning results. The Trust had been established as early as 1860, but its initial policy of buying up slum properties and selling the cleared site to speculative builders proved unpopular and unprofitable, and did not really address itself to the perceived root of the problem–that of tackling the rehousing of the working and poverty-level classes into affordable and decent dwellings. Its policy began to change direction around this period, and it began at last to grasp the nettle and commission its own buildings.

The first municipal housing of this kind was provided in the Saltmarket area of Glasgow by the city architect John Carrick in the late 1880s and 1890s. Although fine tenements of their type, these hardly showed the influence of the free spirit affecting other buildings of this time; rather they display a stiff harking-back to some sanitised Scottish Baronial or Jacobean past with their crow-stepped gables, strapwork and hoodmoulds.

But, from these beginnings, far more full-blooded offspring was to emerge. One of the younger architects who had worked under Carrick was Frank Burnet.

Just a few years after his former employer (and presumably mentor) Carrick was producing the Saltmarket tenements, Burnet, along with Boston and Carruthers, was designing the magnificent red sandstone High Street tenements, again for the City Improvement Trust and built between 1898 and 1901. These really are magnificent tenements; they have it all: turrets, crow steps, bowed frontages, bartizans, parapet balustrades, superbly rising and turning up the slope, with stepped shops at ground-floor level with frontages which have, almost without exception, survived in a way that Saltmarket can only dream of, thanks to the strictures of their District Council landlords.

And almost contemporary with this was another memorable Boston, Burnet and Carruthers scheme—St George's Mansions—displaying the wide eaves and saucer-roofed turrets, full-height oriels and meticulous carving that were to become the hallmark of their work. St George's Mansions were of course always intended as middle-class flats, or mansions as the address confidently suggests.

The bulk of building was, however, undoubtedly undertaken speculatively by private builders and either sold to the mobile middle-class families or rented by the thousands of independent landlords, mostly women to whom property represented their only investment and livelihood. While individual house building was often slow, the tenement system was dependent on speculative, fast building techniques and much credit; even the actual materials were often 'on tick'. It is incredible, then, that so much quality rather than 'jerry-building' was the result.[6]

One reason for this may have been that so many of the new tenements were designed by architects who specialised in tenements to the almost complete exclusion of every-thing else. Most of Glasgow's standard tenements prior to this had been erected mainly by builders (apart, of course, from the upper end of the market, to which the likes of Alexander 'Greek' Thomson catered so well). By this period, however, many of those builders had had sons who had taken the logical step up the social ladder to become architects but who also continued in the work of their parents. The architect John McKellar designed some 640 red sandstone tenements between 1890 and 1900, many of them in Hyndland. Boston, Burnet and Carruthers were not far behind on 540.

That such areas as Hyndland and Dowanhill should have remained wooded hillside for so long may seem hard to believe, but it was only when the improved public transport network had made these areas realistically accessible locations for the new residents that any serious interest was shown by the speculative housebuilder. Mass tenement-builders of the kind providing working-class room and kitchens further down the hill on the flat lands of Partick probably could not afford the extra engineering costs involved in developing a hill site and the attendant roadworks necessary.

Standards, once established in these new areas, were rigorously enforced through clauses in feu contracts, resulting in little or no deviation from the building of these high-quality, middle-class residences. The amenity of the surroundings was also dictated in the original disposal and laying-out of such estates, with land being set aside for open spaces, churches, shops and other community facilities.

It was here that the great wealth of decorative arts was almost orgiastic in profusion: superbly crafted woodwork around doors and stairwells, stained glass anywhere from which a view was not required and where the light would do it most justice, heavy brasswork to door ironmongery and rich plasterwork to reception rooms and hall. By the 1890s, the 'wally close' began to replace whitewashed walls, and some absolutely fabulous Glasgow Style tiles were produced to adorn these, while for those who could afford it Wylie and Lochhead offered exquisite furniture, some of it from the hands of the Glasgow masters at the School of Art.

To conclude, the achievements of the 'second-rate' were quite considerable. They were the achievements of a society that had been well taught and was well-kent in the ways of craftsmanship and innovation and which had proved that neither was incompatible nor contradictory to the other. They succeeded both in beautifying Glasgow and in taking it beyond the bounds of a classical tradition and into the realms of bold, exciting and metropolitan architecture.

Mackintosh himself may have had a slightly ambivalent attitude to these achievements. A distinct note of irritableness is sounded in 1892 when he writes:

> The history of nations is written in stone, but it certainly would be a difficult task to read a history from the architecture of this nation at the present time. We do not build as the ancients did who in each succeeding building tried to carry to further perfection the national type. No, we are a world-acquainted people, who cast aside all prejudice and build now in Greek if we love the Classic, now in Norman if we dote on the Romantic, or if we have travelled show our ill-regulated admiration for foreign beauties by reproducing Swiss chateaux in the most inappropriate positions.[7]

A famous quotation from Mackintosh states:

> There is hope in honest error, none in the icy perfections of the mere stylist.[8]

The word common to both these passages is 'perfection', but used in different contexts, a sort of perfection of national spirit as opposed to a perfection of mere style. Perhaps some of the work of his contemporaries does indeed represent a consciousness of the prevailing 'styles', but in Glasgow, at least, this was so well executed and so generously indulged in, in a civic sense, that it did also come to represent a spirit of the city—one which people felt confident with and identified with. First-rate or world-famous architecture? Perhaps not, but successful and popular in the late Victorian and Edwardian period and still popular today—undoubtedly!

This essay is based on the introductory remarks by Liz Davidson at the Conference 'Mackintosh and his Successful Contemporaries'.

NOTES

1. Published by John Murray as *Mackintosh and his Contemporaries*, ed. Patrick Nuttgens (1988).

2. There is one article by David Walker on 'Mackintosh's Scottish Antecedents' (Nuttgens 1988, op. cit., pp. 32–8). In the Introduction (pp. 6–7), Roger Bilcliffe makes the point that the conference had not been concerned with Mackintosh in his Scottish context.

3. Nikolaus Pevsner *Pioneers of Modern Design*, Museum of Modern Art,

New York (2nd edition 1949). Pevsner deals with Mackintosh in Chapter 6.

4. 'New Buildings in Glasgow', in the *Builders Journal and Architectural Engineer*, 28 November 1906, vol. 24, no. 616.

5. Juliet Kinchin 'Second City of the Empire', in Jude Burkhauser (ed.) *Glasgow Girls: Women in Art and design, 1880–1920* (Cannongate 1990), pp. 28–31.

6. Frank Worsdall *The Glasgow Tenement: A Way of Life* (Chambers 1979; Richard Drew 1989).

7. Charles Rennie Mackintosh 'Untitled Paper on Architecture', in Pamela Robertson (ed.) *Charles Rennie Mackintosh: The Architectural Papers*, (White Cockade, Glasgow 1990,) p. 20.

8. Robertson (1990), op. cit. Quoted by Robertson in Introduction, p. 20.

Mackintosh, Burnet and Modernity

The career of John James Burnet (1857–1938) provides a striking contrast with that of his more famous Glaswegian contemporary, Charles Rennie Mackintosh. He had a wide and varied practice, he was responsible for large-scale projects all over Britain, including Glasgow, Edinburgh and London, and he enjoyed official recognition of his work when he was knighted in 1926. The elevation of Mackintosh into the Modernist Pantheon during the 1930s has tended to obscure Burnet's reputation, but it was not always so.

In a published criticism of an exhibition of architectural designs held in 1923, two drawings by Charles Rennie Mackintosh, appearing rather unexpectedly at that date, were described as 'curiously old-fashioned'. . . . that his work should be represented in an exhibition of contemporary architecture was disconcerting, as disconcerting as would have been the announcement of a new comedy by Oscar Wilde, or a new drawing by Aubrey Beardsley.

So BEGAN the chapter/lecture on 'The End of an Epoch?' by H.S. Goodhart-Rendel in his classic history of *English Architecture since the Regency*.[1] It is one of many quotations which might be used to show that, by the 1920s, Mackintosh was perceived purely as a man of the *fin de siècle* and, as such, rather old-hat. Such judgements help to explain the Mackintosh legend, the story of the misunderstood, progressive figure who abandoned, or was abandoned by, Glasgow in 1914 and who lived on in England and France unknown and unappreciated. This is, of course, partly myth, for the tragedy of Mackintosh is much more complicated and is as much a story of self-destruction as of rejection. There is also the fact that, as Sir John Summerson pointed out long ago, Mackintosh was not forgotten after the Great War but mentioned as a practising architect and one from whom 'the whole modernist movement in European architecture derives' in the 1924 book by the art critic of the London *Times*, Charles Marriott, *Modern English Architecture*—a book which would seem to have the honour of containing the first published illustration of the School of Art.[2]

'Modernist', of course, had certain pejorative or at least alien connotations to an Englishman of the 1920s, and it is evident that Goodhart-Rendel seems to have disliked Mackintosh's work and that of the whole Glasgow School. It is, of course, possible that he was being deliberately provocative in reaction to Mackintosh's promotion as a pioneer of the Modern Movement, but his criticism was not just motivated by prejudice. For Goodhart-Rendel, Mackintosh's work was far too whimsically eccentric, for he wrote that 'there arose in Glasgow a school of young designers who, by putting novelty above all other virtues, achieved results that surprised many and greatly pleased a few. . . . the architectural drawings by Charles Mackintosh, the typical man of the movement, contain much rather childish imitation of the superficial elements in Beardsley's style'. Nor was it just the individualism and self-conscious originality of Mackintosh which offended him, for, while Goodhart-Rendel's own taste was for the rational and often the classical, his own work showed creative dependence upon the Gothic Revival, while his Hay's Wharf Offices in London of 1932 was one of the most idiosyncratic and intelligent 'modern' buildings of its time. Furthermore, he had a deep sympathy for the original 'Rogue architects' of the Victorian age, among whom he included Mackintosh's brilliant and important precursor, James MacLaren 'an architect of very high ability'. Although he dismissed Mackintosh, Goodhart-Rendel praised the 'rational novelty' of MacLaren's Bayswater houses in London, and considered 'that this remarkable work should be so little known is a sad proof that novelty, when it is rational rather than sensational, obtains scanty recognition'.[3]

Nor was Goodhart-Rendel necessarily contemptuous of Glasgow, for he had almost unqualified admiration for the work of Mackintosh's apparent rival, John James Burnet, about whom he wrote an appreciation in 1923, describing him as 'the greatest British architect of the present time'.[4] For many British architects of Goodhart-Rendel's generation (1887–1959, i.e. that of Le Corbusier), Burnet represented order and progress in reaction to the perceived chaotic eclecticism of Victorian and Edwardian architecture. Order was to be restored through the teaching methods of the Ecole des Beaux-Arts, whose evident superiority the buildings of Burnet seemed to exemplify. Later, in 1946, Rendel would call him 'the great Burnet'.

> . . . He was a Frenchified Scotsman, extraordinarily nice, with a tremendous love of order and system. He never lost hold of the essentials and thought no one in England knew anything about them. He used to say that nothing ought to be done without a decision behind it. He had no interest in style as such. . . . He really was a great man, and we were not in the least surprised, when he got the British Museum.[5]

That Burnet was invited down from Scotland to design the extension to the British Museum (Figure 1.1) is, indeed, a key to understanding the architectural politics of the years immediately before and after the Great War. When the building opened in 1914, the *Architectural Review* gave the King Edward VII Galleries extensive coverage and opined that 'The new wing will be counted one of the most important works of English [sic] architecture to which the century has, so far, given birth. . . . No English work of architecture provides us with an effect which is larger or more bold than that produced

1.1 John James Burnet, Edward VII Gallery, British Museum, London 1905–14. Arguably Burnet's most important building. It established his national reputation and demonstrated the superiority of his Beaux-Arts training over British architectural training. (André Goulancourt)

by this lordly array of Ionic columns . . . '.[6] Sixteen years later, A. Trystan Edwards, the lonely defender of Nash's stuccoed Regent Street against rebuilding in monumental Classic Portland stone, could write that

> The King Edward VII Gallery is undoubtedly one of the most impressive architectural compositions which the metropolis can show. It is simple yet splendidly ornate, it is magniloquent without being pompous, it exemplifies the furthest limit of repetitive design yet it is not dull, it reaches to the past and yet its vitality is of today. This design will continue to hold its own and suitably express the function and status of the museum when numerous other facades which at the time of their erection were supposed to represent that elusive thing, the spirit of our century, will seem hopelessly 'passé' and out of date.

This is a significant judgement, for it appeared in Trystan Edwards's introduction to a monograph on *The Architectural Work of Sir John Burnet and Partners* published in 1930–two years after Mackintosh's largely unnoticed death–by 'Masters of Architecture'

Ltd of Geneva in a curious series which included such modern architects as Gocar, Muzio and Kroha. At about the same time, however, the rehabilitation of Mackintosh was beginning as part of the polemical campaign to establish the 'Modern Movement'. In 1927, the architect and journalist Christian Barman tried to persuade Mackintosh to write about modern English architecture (and received the answer that 'I can't write about present-day architecture in England because it doesn't exist').[7]

In 1930, Desmond Chapman-Huston's tribute to Mackintosh was published in the art magazine *Artwork*, but the principal catalyst to the Mackintosh revival was the memorial exhibition held in Glasgow in 1933. This event was even noticed by the *Quarterly* of the Royal Incorporation of Architects in Scotland, which had managed to ignore Mackintosh's death but now published an appreciation by J. Jeffrey Waddell who claimed that 'he has a European reputation together with "Greek" Thomson, and Sir John Burnet–all of Glasgow'.[8] However, the City of Glasgow appears rather less appreciative of her famous son in an article about the city for Civic and Empire Week 1931, written by the President of the Glasgow Institute of Architects, who complacently announced that

> the architecture of Glasgow has the appearance of substantiality associated with its commercial prosperity. The shifting fashions of architecture, as exemplified by much of the building practised at present on the Continent, find little favour here, though, in point of fact, a Glasgow architect, in the person of the late C.R. MacIntosh [sic], was the leader of the Modernist Movement, and 20 years ago he erected buildings in Clasgow, which are regarded to-day as ultra-modern. That the movement has not attained to the extravagance seen in some foreign cities redounds to the credit of Glasgow's common sense.[9]

At the same time, in May 1933, a photograph of the School of Art in the *Architectural Review* accompanied a note about the memorial exhibition, whose text, almost certainly by the Modernist oenophile P. Morton Shand, claimed that 'Mackintosh, unknown and ignored in England, has long been honoured in Scotland and in Europe. He has been called "the father of modern architecture"; a remark which is justified, if by being modern we mean the avoiding of unnecessary decoration and the using of lines as the dominant motif in a building . . . '. Two years later, in the issue for January 1935, Morton Shand discussed Mackintosh in his polemical backwards-history of the Modern Movement entitled 'Scenario for a Human Drama'.

However, Shand could only make Mackintosh seem to fit his definition of 'being modern' by tampering with the evidence, for he could not bear the decorative element in his architecture. In 1933, while promoting the memorial exhibition, Shand simultaneously wrote to Mackintosh's executor, William Davidson, objecting to the inclusion of work by Mackintosh's wife and collaborator, Margaret Macdonald, because

> speaking for myself I rather hope that the emphasis of the exhibition will be on the abiding (the structural) qualities of his work as a great pioneer,

and not on what might be called his 'artistic' contributions, which merely
reflected a happily transient phase of taste. It seems to me clearer than
ever that this side of his work was the result of his wife's influence . . .
Roughly speaking, what will interest the Continent is purely Mackintosh's
architectural-structural work; not the dead and forgotten 'artistic' or 'decorative' frills which so often marred it . . .'[10]

In other words, the 'Art Nouveau' element in Mackintosh which was the focus of the
revival of interest in his works in the 1960s was as much anathema to a modernist like
Shand as it was to contemporary traditionalists. Both shared a dislike of Victorian
decoration in general and 'Spook School' aestheticism in particular.

Shand's discovery of Mackintosh the proto-modernist was rapidly followed by
Nikolaus Pevsner's account of 'one of the most imaginative and brilliant of all young
European architects' in *Pioneers of the Modern Movement from William Morris to Walter
Gropius*. Two years later, in 1938, Burnet—who was eleven years older than Mackintosh—
died at the age of 82, loaded with honours. Even at this late date, however, he could
still also be regarded as a pioneer of modernity. In its obituary, *The Builder* described him
as 'at once a Victorian and a modernist . . . a link between the old and the new, and,
notwithstanding the quality and refinement of his early work, his later work will perhaps
be more memorable for its value in showing the way to an unaffected modern architecture'.[11] So, in the confused 1930s, both Mackintosh and Burnet could be regarded as
pioneers of that nebulous, elusive thing called modern architecture. But little would be
said in praise of Burnet after this time.

This apparent paradox is well summed up by David Walker at the beginning of his
essential article on Burnet published in 1975:

> Since Charles Rennie Mackintosh died, his reputation has gradually
> eclipsed that of Sir John James Burnet. In their lifetime the situation was
> very different. Mackintosh had a small specialised practice, Burnet a large
> and varied one which was the mecca of every aspiring Glasgow apprentice
> . . . Now it is Mackintosh's unique imaginativeness and singleness of
> purpose which is valued, and the antipathy between the two artists has
> lived on after them to Burnet's discredit.

And Walker hinted at the reason for this when he went on to note how, 'paradoxically,
Burnet's own success has put him at a disadvantage, for Burnet as a modernist has been
obscured by his spectacular skill as a stylist'.[12]

Style is, in fact, the key to the paradox, for style—or, rather, the perceived rejection
of historic styles—obsessed those who constructed the modern historiography of late
Victorian and Edwardian architecture. Pevsner, in 1936, could write of the School of
Art that 'not a single feature here is derived from period styles'—a judgement surely
denied by unprejudiced inspection of the building and certainly not sustained by more
recent analyses of Mackintosh's architecture.[13] That Thomas Howarth, Mackintosh's

principal biographer, interpreted his architecture in such terms as implicit in the title of his 1952 book, *Charles Rennie Mackintosh and the Modern Movement*. But Howarth recognised that the relationship of Mackintosh to Burnet cannot be understood in simplistic, progressive terms, when he wrote how

> The Burnets dominated the architectural field in the West of Scotland during the last quarter of the century, and inevitably set a standard—and a fashion—to which all consciously or unconsciously subscribed. Though Mackintosh deprecated their Classical enterprises, no less than they disapproved of him and his circle, he had a profound regard for their masterly handling of form, and he closely followed their work in the native idiom.[14]

Indeed, as David Walker has shown, details derived from Burnet appear—transmuted—in Mackintosh's designs.

Unfortunately, many historians cannot see the form for the style. Seeking 'free style' or non-stylar buildings as pointers towards the future, they fail to appreciate that a design expressed in a conventional historical language may still be innovative in terms of planning, spatial organisation and construction—which was conspicuously the case with John James Burnet. For with Burnet, as with any intelligent product of the Beaux-Arts, style was not an absolute but a language for formal expression to be chosen for its appropriateness, and he was equally adept with the Classical and the Gothic.[15] As Goodhart-Rendel put it, 'He had no interest in style as such' and so was not concerned with producing a distinctly 'modern' language of expression. As a result, he has been lumped together with many much less innovative Classicists who flourished in Edwardian Britain. Poor Burnet has suffered from a blinkered and superficial approach to architecture which is interested only in appearance rather than substance.

A selective obsession with so-called 'free style' architecture as a progressive movement at the turn of the century informs many of the essays in Alastair Service's compendium, *Edwardian Architecture and its Origins*. Characteristic is a sentence in Nicholas Taylor's account of 'Sir Albert Richardson: A Classic Case of Edwardianism' (in reality, an intelligently progressive Classicist) as 'a casebook for historians on the perplexing collapse of the English "free" style around 1905 and the re-establishment of classicism in Edwardian architecture'.[16] There is, in fact, nothing perplexing about it once it is understood that, soon after the beginning of the new century, there arose a widespread reaction against the undisciplined individualism of 'free style' architecture in favour of the more logical and rational approach to new methods and problems represented by Classicism. Enjoyable as it always is for posterity, extreme individualism may fail fo provide universal answers to the general architectural problems faced by any age.

Though it much interests historians, true originality is difficult to find at any time, and only a very small number of architects ever have genuinely new ideas. As Mackintosh's mentor, W.R. Lethaby, once said, 'no great art is only one man deep'. Periods of intense creativity are also difficult, if not impossible, to sustain for long and, all over Europe, that remarkable and exuberant experimentation with *l'art nouveau* and *Jugendstil* was waning by 1905, to be succeeded by more sober, more Classical approaches. This is evident with Victor Horta, with Josef Olbrich and, especially, with Peter Behrens. Howarth, among others, rightly observes that Mackintosh's achievement was confined to an 'extraordinarily short period of intense activity . . . little more than a decade' from 1896 to 1906.[17] Give or take a year, the same could be said of Horta, or, indeed, of Edwin Lutyens in his 'progressive' vernacular mode. But Lutyens changed, of course, discovering the 'High Game' of Classicism which informs most of his subsequent, conspicuously creative work.

For critics like Pevsner, however, Lutyens's development from a Surrey vernacular to Renaissance Classicism was a retrogressive step; 'England herself,' he wrote in 1936, 'receded into an eclectic Neo-Classicism, of great dignity sometimes, but with hardly any bearing on present-day problems and needs'. However, at the time, America seemed the most potent source of new ideas, and it can be argued that possibly Lutyens's brilliant and mannered Classicism and certainly Burnet's abstracted Grand Manner had considerable bearing on the problem of designing a multi-storeyed, steel-framed commercial building in a tight urban context. Indeed, in a footnote, Pevsner cited Kodak House (Figure 1.2) in Kingsway, London, a very American design by Burnet with Thomas Tait, as one of the 'few factories and office buildings' in England that were 'exceptional'.[18]

The mistake was to regard Mackintosh in isolation as a lonely pioneer. John Betjeman realised this when he wrote in 1952 how 'two great architects, C.R. Mackintosh and George Walton . . . are wrongly, I think, heralded as pioneers of modern architecture. They now seem to me to belong to the *art nouveau* of the 1890s . . .'[19] But the necessary revisionism really began with Robert Macleod's 1968 biography, which concludes that Mackintosh was 'a last and remote efflorescence of a vital British tradition which reached back to Pugin. . . . With his pursuit of the "modern", his love of the old, and his obsessive individuality, he was one of the last and one of the greatest of the Victorians'.[20] But if Mackintosh was a Victorian individualist, where does that leave Burnet? His approach was very different, as he stated in 1923 when awarded the RIBA's Royal Gold Medal. 'If it is true that an architect is here to serve his day and generation—and I think he is, and that it is at once his duty and his pleasure—what qualities,' asked Burnet, 'must he not possess if he is to master all his clients' requirements and produce a building efficient for its purpose, suitable for its size, and so simple in its conception that it appears a perfect harmony, created without effort, a simple and beautiful monument to the integrity and purpose of the generation in which it was built! There is no spurious originality in such work, no conscious individuality on the part of the designer . . .'[21]

Unlike Mackintosh, who—for whatever reason—retreated into embittered isolation as

1.2 John James Burnet and Thomas Smith Tait, Kodak House, Kingsway, London, 1910–11. An American-inspired, steel-framed commercial building demonstrating the modernity of Burnet's designs at this time. (André Goulancourt)

an unappreciated genius, Burnet continued to serve his day and generation. If Mackintosh was the individualist, Burnet was the collective rationalist, the self-abnegating synthesist (distinct and personal though his interpretation of the Classical tradition was). Both are necessary in a creative architectural culture. Indeed, as David Walker wrote in 1977 in reviewing the second edition of Howarth's book, 'there were then *two* rival and quite independent schools of highly progressive architecture in the city'.[22] If Mackintosh and Burnet are taken together as two aspects of a Glasgow phenomenon, then their careers form a continuum which parallels the individual careers of, say , Horta and Lutyens. Ironically, despite Mackintosh's adherence to English Arts and Crafts ideals, his intensely personal style left little scope for other artists, while Burnet's work was conspicuous for a successful collaboration between the architect and sculptors such as George Frampton. And it was Burnet who did much more to grapple with the constructional and planning problems posed by the technology and building types of his day. Mackintosh's construction was almost always traditional—the School of Art is built like a contemporary Glasgow tenement—while it was Burnet who met the challenges posed by iron, steel and reinforced concrete. Macintosh's Scotland Street School, which is so intriguingly reminiscent of Gropius's seminal Werkbund Exhibition Factory, certainly reveals a wonderfully direct use of steel, but it is scarcely innovative in structural terms.

Goodhart-Rendel recognised this when he claimed, albeit rather petulantly, that 'there is no evidence . . . that the Glasgow group had any prevision of the new methods of construction that afterwards retrospectively gave meaning to some of their meaning-less innovations, and it is rash to claim that the laboratory culture of Glasgow peculiari-ties abroad resulted in anything more important than amusement.'[23] But Goodhart-Rendel was wrong, in that he neglected Mackintosh's friend and sympathiser, the younger James Salmon. Salmon may have lacked Mackintosh's originality in decorative terms, but he has the honour of designing the first reinforced concrete building in central Glasgow— Lion Chambers—while his 'Hatrack' building in St Vincent Street is such an intelligent and fanciful architectural treatment of a steel frame on a difficult, confined site that it establishes him as a major architectural talent—not just in the city's 'laboratory culture' but also in European terms.

And not far behind Salmon came Burnet and his sometime partner (also Paris-trained), J.A. Campbell, who were the real architects of the distinctive character of Edwardian Glasgow, to which—despite the brilliance of his 'Daily Record' building with its recessed and stylised Classical mouldings designed to maximise light in narrow alleys—Mackin-tosh's career was somehow tangential. Two buildings by Burnet of 1899, Atlantic Chambers and Waterloo Chambers, both employ steel frames behind their enigmatic, complex and mannered stone facades. But Burnet's most impressive and experimental building was McGeoch's warehouse of 1905. This huge building had stone facades of a rationally abstracted Classical design inspired by rather higher American buildings, behind which stood a steel frame supporting some of the first reinforced concrete slabs to be cast in Britain *in situ*. 'McGeoch's,' wrote Gomme and Walker, 'marks an impressive moment of the functional tradition in Britain, when the satisfaction to be gained from the straightforward and compromising expression of constructional materials was being rediscovered.'[24] Its demolition in 1971 (along with the mutilation of the Wallace Scott Tailoring Institute factory at Cathcart) has seriously distorted our picture of architectural developments in Edwardian Glasgow.

It is often hinted that there was no love lost between these two great Glaswegians, Mackintosh and Burnet. No doubt Burnet disapproved of the younger man as an architectural influence, but it is also possible that the antipathy was personal—just as Burnet broke with Campbell because of the latter's heavy drinking. Unfortunately, so much that has been written about Mackintosh is tiresomely coy about the personal factors that may have been responsible for the eventual tragedy of his career. What is certain is that while no influence of 'The Four' is evident in Burnet's work, Mackintosh certainly adopted hints from Burnet, transmuting and developing them in his own personal creative manner. We know that the young Mackintosh admired certain of Burnet's buildings, but these would seem to be the few that were more English in character and most influenced by Norman Shaw.[25] As much of the Mackintosh legend depends upon English indifference to his achievement, there is a certain irony in the fact that while Mackintosh was well aware of the work of advanced English Goths and Arts and Crafts designers, it was Burnet, whose sources of inspiration mostly came from Paris, New York and Chicago, who had by far the most impact on England. But, of course, while Mackintosh's style was self-consciously and distinctively Scottish, Burnet strove for a more anonymous international character.

A certain debt to Burnet is evident in Mackintosh's supreme masterpiece, the School of Art. David Walker has pointed out how Burnet's characteristic flattened and wide architrave mouldings are employed by Mackintosh on the East Wing, together with other Classical elements such as guttae, of which he was particularly fond and which he used with deliberate Mannerist perversity (Figures 1.3 and 1.4). Another feature of the building which has received less attention are the two lengths of broad projecting eaves cornice on the North Front (Figure 1.5). This, of a Tuscan simplicity which acts as a satisfactory termination to the flat-roofed studios, is remarkable in that it neither returns at its ends not reaches to the corners of the building. A similar projecting cornice, roofing an eaves gallery and divided by a chimney, appears at the top of Burnet's (later) Atlantic Chambers, for a cornice which stops short of the full width of a building is, of course, a logical answer to the problem of a Classical street frontage which is contained by adjoining buildings of equal or potentially similar height.

The School of Art, however, is a free-standing building on three sides, so there was no reason for Mackintosh to cut back his cornice before the northern corners other than

1.3 Charles Rennie Mackintosh, detail of east façade of Glasgow School of Art, 1898–9.
Some of Mackintosh's work appears to have been influenced by Burnet. Compare the flat,
wide mouldings of this doorway with those in Figure 1.4. (Author)

his evident desire to give the end elevations a distinct, castle-like character by carrying
up the wall higher to a parapet. Possibly this device is anticipated by a less dominant
cornice on the Glasgow Herald building of 1893–4, which stops to allow the dramatic
corner turret to run up without interruption. But a more interesting precedent is the
more prominent cornice on the taller, rear block of the Glasgow Savings Bank on the
corner of Glassford and Ingram Streets. Here, even before the building was heightened
by Burnet with a colonnaded eaves gallery, the cornices stopped short of the distinctive
rusticated and facetted corners which rise up sheer above cornice and balustrade to form
chimneys.[26] Burnet first visited the United States in 1896, and this feature could possibly
have been derived from an American building: the Bowery Savings Bank of 1895 by
McKim, Mead and White (which, again, is a free-standing building not confined by
neighbours). Whatever its source, this cornice treatment soon developed into the
characteristic Burnet treatment of a Classical order, whether implicit or fully expressed,
terminated by higher corner pylons or chimneys; its appearance on the School of Art,
albeit much simplified, cannot be mere coincidence.

1.4 John James Burnet, doorcase of Athenaeum building, Glasgow, 1886. An early work by Burnet which typifies his handling of doorcase mouldings. This kind of treatment certainly influenced Mackintosh. (Author)

The East Wing of the School of Art was built in 1898–9. By the time the West Wing was built, in 1907–9, to a completely revised design (which, again, ignores the line of the dominating North Front cornice), the Burnet Classical influence had been largely (but not entirely) replaced by a stylised and smooth Gothic verticality which, as Summerson has pointed out, may well have been inspired by the 'mannered modernity' of Charles Holden's Bristol Reference Library and the London work of that brilliant exiled Glaswegian Classicist, John Belcher's partner, J.J. Joass.[27] But, in considering the progressive or 'modern' nature of the School of Art, what is interesting is the fact, so often considered to be evidence of Mackintosh's lonely struggle against an uncomprehending or hostile establishment, that the completed building seems not to have been published until 1924. This could conceivably be owing to the lengthy interval since the Honeyman and Keppie design was first chosen in 1897; possibly it reflects the notoriously blinkered attitude of the London architectural papers to Glasgow. But the possibility must also be considered that Mackintosh did not want it published—why did he not prepare a drawing of the West Wing as he did for the Scotland Street School? Even in

1.5 Charles Rennie Mackintosh, detail of north front of Glasgow School of Art, 1897–9.
The projecting eaves cornice is a feature which also starts to appear in Burnet's work at
around the same date. It was developed by Burnet into something of a trademark. (Author)

1909, he would surely have had no difficulty getting an illustration into *The Studio* or a
German magazine.

The cruel fact was that architecture had changed over those dozen years—and not
necessarily in a retrogressive manner. By the time the School was finished, it must have
seemed a little out of date even to Mackintosh, who was himself preparing to change
direction. David Walker has noticed this, writing in 1977 how,

> in the library wing of the School of Art in 1907–9 Mackintosh absorbed a
> limited number of Viennese-inspired motifs into his own style and
> produced the finest work of his own career. As a large building on an
> exceptional site it represented an opportunity not likely to recur, a
> triumph impossible to live up to; and one strongly suspects that the heavy
> drinking which began about 1907 was symptomatic of a chronic indecision
> as to whether or not he should cling to his own decorative style of subtly
> curving natural forms, which time was slowly but surely passing by, or
> adopt the severe rectilinear geometric idiom of Hoffmann and his friends
> in Vienna: it was no light step for a man who had received a hero's

welcome in that city to become a follower rather than a leader. Yet that is exactly what he did . . .'[28]

In other words, Mackintosh himself responded to the Classicising tendencies in Europe, but in a distinct, non-historicist manner which now seems to anticipate 'Art Deco'. Yet there was an even more immediate explanation for Mackintosh feeling disctinctly uncomfortable by 1909, for his style was regarded as passé even by the students at the School of Architecture in his own building.

It is not surprising, in the city in which 'Greek' Thomson was remembered and revered, that the Classical tradition should always have been strong at the School since the foundation of the Architectural Section in 1887. It would have been encouraged by Burnet's protégé, the brilliant draughtsman Alexander McGibbon, as Director of Architectural Studies.[29] In 1904, French influence dramatically increased when Eugene Bourdon was nominated by J.L. Pascal in Paris as an architect to report on design teaching in Glasgow and unify two separate schools. He is now rather forgotten, but the presence in Scotland of this Frenchman who had worked in New York and who was two years younger than Mackintosh can only have been distressing to him, as Bourdon represented what was truly *avant-garde* in the Edwardian architectural scene: the attempt to follow the methods and ideals of the Ecole des Beaux-Arts. And behind that attempt in Glasgow was Pascal's devoted pupil, J.J. Burnet, a governor of the School.

Bourdon would seem to have been intoduced expressly to counter the Mackintosh influence—or what Burnet later described as 'spurious originality' and 'conscious individuality on the part of the designer'. Even allowing for wartime hyperbole and prejudice, this is clearly indicated by a Glasgow obituary which appeared after his death, on the Somme, in 1916.

> For it was to battle he came amongst us, to wage war upon sheer mediocrity and upon a strong cult of eccentricity in architecture which, strangely enough, emanated from Austria and Germany [sic!]—enemies alike of freedom and justice and of the spirit of beauty which evolves through the ages and carries forward the great work of tradition. . . . there was at first in our minds a certain resentment against the teachings of a foreigner, a prejudice against the very principles for which he contended. We, the generation whom he called to his standard, heard grave doubts expressed by our elders, and, with our inherent insularity, suspected his methods. Some of us began with a definite aversion to French architecture. Its gaiety shocked our more sober tastes; we were too young then and too untrained to see below the superabundance of ornament and the elaborate and intricate manipulation of form and line sound principles of proportion and that fitness in the use of materials upon which all fine work is based. . . . Then slowly it dawned upon our understanding that the few men who were our own national leaders in the art of building—our heroes—owed a great debt to their time of study in Paris . . .'[30]

The depth of the reaction to the eclecticism and individualism of late Victorian architecture in the early years of this century can scarcely be exaggerated. Following on from the 'Profession or an Art?' controversy of 1891, a widespread desire for a systematised architectural education in schools to supplant the old tradition of articled pupillage encouraged an uncritical admiration for the Ecole des Beaux-Arts—especially after it was appreciated that the widely-admired modern Classical commercial and institutional buildings in the United States were the work of Paris-trained men like Hastings and McKim. It culminated in the establishment of the First Atelier in London in 1913. This 'Entente Cordiale' in design education was promoted by young heads of school in three institutions in particular by Mackintosh's enemy (for personal reasons), the 'pompous bounder' C.H. Reilly (1874–1947) at Liverpool after 1904; by Robert Atkinson (1883–1952) at the Architectural Association in London after 1912; and by Bourdon in Glasgow.[31]

Alan Powers, the historian of British architectural education at the turn of the century, has noted that

> only in Glasgow could a French architect have been appointed head of a school at this date, and the choice was particularly fortunate. Bourdon's American experiences put him in direct touch with the work which Reilly was to discover like a revelation a few years later. Unlike some of the English Beaux-Arts enthusiasts, he realised the danger of transplanting the French style undigested, but he knew more thoroughly than they did the French educational method for architects, and believed that this could have beneficial effects.[32]

The effect of the Ecole des Beaux-Arts is widely misunderstood in Britain in that it is interpreted in purely stylistic terms. But while Parisian influences may be detected in Burnet's earlier work, the real effect of Beaux-Arts training was in terms of method rather than style. Again, to reiterate Goodhart-Rendel, 'he had no interest in style as such' (although perhaps it required this sympathetic Englishman to point out 'how positively if indefinably Scottish all his work is, never more so that when it savours faintly of Paris . . .'[33] In his history of the period in which began his own career, Goodhart-Rendel perspicaciously explained how the revived taste for the neo-Classical—manifested by an enthusiasm for the architecture of C.R. Cockerell at both Liverpool and the Architectural Association and the publication of Richardson's *Monumental Classic Architecture in Great Britain and Ireland during the XVIIIth & XIXth Centuries* in 1914—could be interpreted as a desire for the '*architectural*' in opposition to the Picturesque which underlay so much Victorian and Edwardian design. Goodhart-Rendel wrote in 1953:

> In the ten years preceding the last war, architecturalism—organised arch-
> itecture, that is to say—was much reviled by young and enthusiastic utilita-
> rians. In this it is now clear that they were barking up the wrong tree,
> having mistaken the enemy. Architecturalism as it was embodied in the

> teaching of the Ecole des Beaux-Arts was absolutely practical and rational in method, although based, no doubt, on aesthetic and moral hypotheses that material utilitarians would reject. Agreeing to differ upon these, the neo-Classicist and the utilitarian should have been able to work harmoniously along parallel lines, each accepting as axiomatic that all architectural ends, whether aesthetic or physical, must be attained by means that are logical and direct. What every logical utilitarian should violently abhor is not the neo-Classical but the Picturesque. The Picturesque that flouts reason . . .[34]

This convergence between the neo-Classical and the utilitarian is, surely, precisely what the career of Sir John Burnet exemplifies, and explains why his firm was able to evolve into Sir John Burnet, Tait and Lorne and to produce some of the most rational Modern Movement buildings in Britain between the wars. That style, as such, was unimportant was also maintained by Bourdon. 'I make a departure between Art and Art Education', he wrote in 1908.

> Art may be classic or not, traditionalist or not; the decision stands with practising national artists; but in all cases Art education, like any education, should be classic, i.e., based upon the tradition. . . . I have brought here, in Architecture, not French architecture as a few fancy, but the architectural tradition, the old Greek tradition, transplanted to Rome, modified in the Gothic, renewed at the Renaissance. My students in practice will make 'classic' or 'modern' art. That is their own affair.[35]

But as Alan Powers notes, 'this doctrine is so alien to English architectural thinking that it had little chance of being understood, and even less of being generally adopted, but the Glasgow school did encourage it . . .'.[36]

Mackintosh's art, however, seems to have been regarded neither as 'classic' nor 'modern' but as largely irrelevant to architectural progress, and a younger Glasgow generation's attitude to him is suggested by comments in *The Vista*, the magazine published by the Glasgow School of Architecture Club, started up by Bourdon. In 1910, H.L.H. [Honeyman?], in an article on 'Truism' or Truth, joked that 'Truly, modern draughtsmanship has much to answer for; its Father was the Evil one, its Mother the Renaissance, and its Nurse the Gothic Revival. In the School of Art itself we see beautiful steel lintels hidden behind lathing and cement sanded and painted stone-colour . . .'[37] A nice irony, that, to have poked fun at Mackintosh for deception, especially as the Beaux-Arts system, although concerned with fine draughtsmanship, was always opposed to the picturesque and possibly misleading perspective drawing at which Mackintosh excelled.

The preceding year, an anonymous correspondent reviewed the newly completed School of Art building (the Editor was James R. Adamson, who gave his address as 'c/o John Burnet & Son') and 'wondered if Mr Mackintosh felt forlorn or relieved at having this child of his imagination off his hands. Of course that would depend on whether it was a child of joy or sorrow to him, a prodigy or a freak. In our opinion—but, silence is the better part of discretion. There are, however, things which can be said about the child. The finest is, that it expresses what it professes to be. There are about it elements of mystery quite typical of the teaching of art . . .' But while the student grudgingly praised it as 'a plain building' and because 'above all things, it is an interesting building, and this is the next best thing to being beautiful', he clearly had little patience with the Mackintosh *style*.

> Mr Mackintosh aimed at doing something bizarre, we would congratulate him on his success while condemning it on principle. But we think better of him, and it may be that Mackintoshian ideals are not to be expressed in the ordinary language of architecture. . . . While the strength of Mr Mackintosh's architecture lies perhaps in its mystery, his system of decoration has its strength or weakness in its obviousness. His method is one of permutations and combinations of simple forms. This algebraic basis must account for the lack of romance in new art interiors. Coming fresh to the system, one finds interest in noticing that the details of a repeated ornamental motive are never the same, then it grows clear that the motive itself was selected in order that its internal arrangement might allow of endless different combinations, so that once the motive is selected an office boy or a trained cat can do the rest . . .[38]

Much can be read into this article, especially when the author writes that 'notwithstanding the play of fancy (or is it humour) shown, the design is a serious effort—maybe tragically so!' Student opinion is always a reliable guide to the latest fashion, so this cannot have been pleasant for Mackintosh to read. Having himself been a brilliant student and been taken up as a prodigy at an early age, having been feted abroad and possessing no little personal vanity, for Charles Rennie Mackintosh—the *avant-garde* phenomenon of Glasgow of the 1890s—to have lost touch with a younger generation and to be jokingly patronised by a student critic must have been almost intolerable. Perhaps it was this, rather than the continuing hostility of older architects like Burnet, which indicated to Mackintosh that there was little future in Glasgow for his architecture. No wonder the poor man went into a decline.

Now it must be admitted that, despite Burnet and Bourdon, the Beaux-Arts approach soon became associated merely with promoting a particular style—a monumental, rather American Classicism—and that Bourdon's teaching failed to produce any architects of great distinction. There was J.M. Whitelaw, who died young in 1913; there was A.T. Scott, who later became Sir Herbert Baker's partner and successor; and there was Richard Gunn, who went on to design the most magnificently American building in interwar Glasgow, James Miller's Bank of Scotland in St Vincent Street. The irony is that the modernity of Burnet's practice after the Great War was achieved by assistants and partners who were usually *not* products of pure Beaux-Arts methods—Thomas Tait had been at the Glasgow School of Art before Bourdon arrived, while Francis Lorne enjoyed a traditional British training. It is also undeniable that it was individualists like Mackintosh who were able to invest buildings with the poetry which is so lacking in so much twentieth-century production, whether 'architectural' or 'utilitarian'. Nevertheless, it was the aura of the Beaux-Arts and its perceived superiority to English amateurism which was largely responsible for Burnet being invited to extend the British Museum in 1904.

Burnet was chosen by the Trustees of the Museum from a list of architects furnished by the RIBA. It was a victory which redeemed Glasgow's shame for commissioning a fashionable London architect, without competition, to design the University back in the 1860s, even if Burnet's establishment of a London office in 1905 might now seem to symbolise the beginning of Glasgow's long, sad economic decline. What Burnet's appointment clearly indicated was that no London architect was up to the job, and English architects were in awe of the sophistication and grasp of essentials manifested by the Beaux-Arts-trained Glaswegian. They were not disappointed when the North Wing of the Museum was completed. In 1913, the *Architectural Review* was delighted that, as with the Parthenon,

> considerable attention has been given to the correction of optical illusion, all the columns being inclined inwards from the vertical axis to the extent of 2¼", thus avoiding the appearance of leaning towards the street; the columns are also irregularly spaced, the distance between each progressively increasing towards the centre from either end, thus avoiding the appearance of crushing the middle of the facade.

Others noticed that, as Burnet had continued Smirke's giant Ionic order but engaged it on a chord rather than the diameter, this backward tilt avoided a difficult conjunction between the fluting and the wall surface. What Englishman (other than Lutyens) would have thought of that, let alone bothered to carry it out?

The following year, the magazine announced that

> the interior is admirably arranged, and Mr Burnet reveals his complete mastery of the art of planning. . . . Mr Burnet is to be congratulated upon having achieved a great architectural triumph, for he has endowed a highly complex structure with the appearance of simplicity.[39]

Interestingly, what English commentators seemed least happy with is the most distinctive and most Glaswegian feature of the monumental Ionic facade. This was the central entrance which, with its typically flattened architraves and Mannerist entablature, breaks through the level of the podium set by Smirke almost a century earlier. They could not, it seems, appreciate how exquisitely Burnet had judged the status of this porch, for it was a back entrance which yet deserved some dignity. It was placed at ground level, and, as the podium doorcase, Burnet cut into the horizontal line of his column bases with a disregard for the rules that showed he was no pedant.

Inside, Burnet also showed that he was a master in the handling of space as well as in

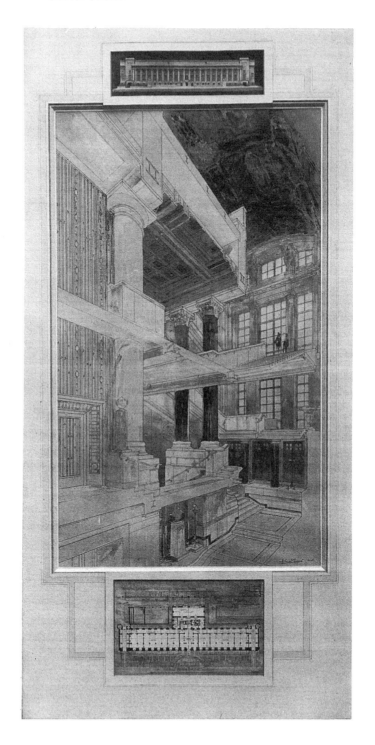

precise and thoughtful detailing. The visitor enters a low entrance hall, which could seem oppressive if it were not relieved by an oculus allowing appreciation of the spaciousness of the gallery above, with its ceiling modulated by a careful hierarchy of trabeation. The axial vista from the entrance ends with a small bust of Edward VII, and here the confined space ends for, to the right, one of the finest staircases in London dramatically opens out (Figure 1.6). It rises in a space reaching the whole height of the building under a gilded barrel vault and is articulated by gigantic columns of different orders rising from subtly different levels which thread unhindered through three floors. And this imposing, heroic circulation space is given added interest and unity by a richly-treated iron and bronze lift cage. The seemingly effortless resolution of the complexity of both construction and space here is shown in the magnificent cutaway interior perspectives exhibited by Burnet at the Royal Academy in 1912.[40] Mackintosh is rightly praised for his masterly handling of planes of space, but it can only be stylistic prejudice that blinds modern commentators to the equally dramatic and subtle spatial effects created by Burnet in Bloomsbury.

Sadly, Burnet's other fine interior in the British Museum's new wing, the North Library on axis from the Round Reading Room, has been altered and spoiled. Originally, this double-height galleried space was articulated by a consciously Mannerist Ionic order which broke forward to support a densely-trabeated ceiling. If secondary to the spatial complexity and gloriously inventive detail of Mackintosh's contemporary Library in the Glasgow School of Art, it was nontheless a deeply impressive achievement. Also deserving of praise are Burnet's surviving details in the building, such as the direct and noble handling of staircases with simple marble panels sometimes fixed with bronze rosettes, flush with the marble top surface and enlivened by a carefully-modelled bronze handrail of cobra-like form. Burnet could handle materials in a manner that was at once dignified and straightforward, creating a style which succeeded in being both sympathetically Classical and yet modern in feeling. Few buildings in Britain are as well made as the King Edward VII Galleries, which is without doubt the finest Edwardian public building in London. It is quite as good as any contemporary work by Behrens or Wagner.

In recognition of his achievement in Bloomsbury, Burnet was knighted in 1914. That same year saw Mackintosh's pathetic exile from his native city. The careers of the two Glaswegians could not be more different. To the modern sensibility, informed by the *avante-garde* interpretation of art history, lonely rejection owing to public incomprehension is more attractive than worldly success. But it is both the tragedy and the triumph of the art of architecture that it has to be built, so that Burnet's success in producing

---

1.6 John James Burnet, sectional perspective of the staircase in the Edward VII Gallery at the British Museum, London, 1912. This drawing shows that, like Mackintosh, Burnet was a master of handling space. (Royal Academy of Arts, London)

great architecture which fulfilled the needs of his time must not be belittled. Compromise is the essence of architecture; to keep abreast of current developments rather
than to hold on regardless to a particular vision is essential in a creative architect, and
part of Burnet's achievement was to encourage the development of a modern architectural idiom. This was recognised by one of his obituarists, who wrote that 'to
architects Sir John Burnet's great qualities were his recognition of the limits of the
individual in modern architectural practice on a large scale and his ability to move with
the times . . .'[41]

The history of twentieth-century architecture is one of tension between a personal
expression by certain inspired individuals and the need for a collective approach at a time
of rapid technological change and functional complexity (which was precisely the essence
of the quarrel between Henri van de Velde and Hermann Muthesius in the Deutsche
Werkbund just before the Great War). At the time, Mackintosh's personal style seemed
to offer few lessons for the new century; although he was a partner in a successful and
respected Glasgow practice, his work was always jealously individual and, after the
painful break-up of 1913, he left no heirs. As a potential influence, Mackintosh's work
then seemed dead, and it is possible that his evident disinclination to resume a career
as an architect was a recognition that he had nothing new to say. Some artists burn out
rapidly while others can sustain their creativity; some architects live too long while
others do not live long enough. Burnet lived on, but at first managed to move with the
times. By running a large office with a shared approach to design, he permitted men like
Tait and Lorne to develop a 'stripped Classic' manner into a distinctly modern idiom.
In 1914, old though he was, Burnet was still a man with a future, and his Kodak Building
of 1910–11 in London—probably designed with Tait—provided a useful and elegant model
for countless commercial buildings over the next two decades. That, for the 1920s at
any rate, was 'modern architecture'.

To make these comparisons between these two remarkable Glaswegians is not to
attempt to restore Burnet's reputation at the expense of Mackintosh's. Both men had
great, and complementary, strengths. While Mackintosh could not handle large,
modern, steel-framed buildings with Burnet's aplomb, the elder man lacked Mackintosh's extraordinary ability to transmute conventional forms into something new,
appropriate, decorative and personal, while making simple materials sing. What this
comparison is intended to show is that the idea of modernity in the twentieth century
is by no means simple and static, that historians are as much creatures of fashion in their
judgements as anyone else, and that the architectural scene in Edwardian Glasgow was
more complex and subtle than is generally recognised. Perhaps the last word should be
given to Burnet's greatest pupil, his fellow Scot, Thomas Tait, whose modernist
credentials—as the architect of the Silver End houses and the designer of the Empire
Exhibition in Glasgow—were impeccable; for he wrote, at the time of Burnet's death,

that 'although Sir John could never tolerate what is understood as ''Art nouveau'', with its spurious originality, he was one of the most modern architects of his time . . .'.[42]

Mackintosh School of Architecture

ACKNOWLEDGEMENTS
I have benefited from the advice of Dr Alan Powers, Dr James Macaulay, Alan Crawford and Professor Andrew MacMillan in the preparation of this chapter.

NOTES
  1. H.S. Goodhart-Rendel, *English Architecture since the Regency*, 1953, p. 223 (edition edited by Alan Powers, 1989). The text was originally written for the Slade Lectures given in Oxford in 1934, and published much later with little revision. Goodhart-Rendel was in fact quoting his own notice in the *Architectural Review*, January 1923, pp. 26–31, of 'An Exhibition of Contemporary British Architecture' held at the RIBA in December 1922.
  2. John Summerson, 'The British Contemporaries of Frank Lloyd Wright' in *Acts of the Twentieth International Congress of the History of Art*, New York, 1963, and reprinted in Summerson's *The Unromantic Castle*, 1990. It is interesting to note that Summerson recalls that when he first visited Glasgow in 1926, Mackintosh 'was still alive and his works were remembered, if at all, only as something quite out-moded and not worth a thought or glance. Thomson was Glasgow's architect hero.' See 'A Trip to the North 1926' in *Macmag 16*, the magazine of the Mackintosh School of Architecture, Glasgow, 1991, p. 56.
  3. Goodhart-Rendel, op. cit., pp. 196–7.
  4. Goodhart-Rendel in *The Architect's Journal*, 27 June 1923.
  5. Nikolaus Pevsner, 'Goodhart-Rendel's Roll-Call', in *The Architectural Review*, October 1965, pp. 259–64, reprinted in Alastair Service (ed.) *Edwardian Architecture and its Origins*, 1975.
  6. *AR* May 1913.
  7. Letter quoted in Alastair Moffat (ed.) *Remembering Charles Rennie Mackintosh*, 1989, p. 138.
  8. *RIAS Quarterly*, no 42, 1933, p. 14. Chapman-Huston's article on Mackintosh in *Artwork* was noticed in the *Quarterly* no 32, 1930, p. 107, and reprinted in the RIBA's *Handbook to the British Architects Conference at Glasgow* in 1935.
  9. George A. Boswell, 'Glasgow Architecture' in *The Book of Glasgow: Civic and Empire Week*, 1931, p. 69.
  10. Letters from Shand to Davidson, 31 March and 7 April 1933, in the Hunterian Art Gallery, quoted in Jude Burkhauser (ed.) *'Glasgow Girls': Women in Art and Design 1880–1920*, 1990, pp. 23 and 25.
  11. *The Builder*, 8 July 1938.

12. David Walker, 'Sir John James Burnet', in Alastair Service (ed.) *Edwardian Architecture and its Origins*, 1975, p. 193.

13. Nikolaus Pevsner, *Pioneers of the Modern Movement from William Morris to Walter Gropius*, 1936, p. 158. For Mackintosh's sources, see David Walker, 'Charles Rennie Mackintosh', *Architectural Review*, November 1968, reprinted in A. Service, op. cit., and James Macaulay, 'Elizabethan Architecture' and David Walker, 'Mackintosh on Architecture', in Pamela Robertson (ed.) *Charles Rennie Mackintosh: The Architectural Papers*, 1990.

14. Thomas Howarth, *Charles Rennie Mackintosh and the Modern Movement*, 1977 edition, p. 55.

15. Burnet evidently baffled Pevsner, who wondered, in his introduction to Andor Gomme and David Walker, *Architecture of Glasgow*, 1968, 'How could a man develop from a Beaux-Arts training in Paris to the bold and wholly convincing angular neo-Baroque of the narrow front of the Athenaeum Theatre of 1891 and end with the calm and competent classical Edward VII's Galleries of the British Museum on the one hand with the "Early Modern" Kodak Building in London and the Wallace Scott tailoring factory at Cathcart on the other?', evidently unable to accept that his Beaux-Arts training might be the key to this paradox.

16. Service, op. cit., p. 445. This article was first published in the *Architectural Review* in 1966. To be fair, Taylor also recognised that Richardson's late masterpiece, Bracken House, London, of 1954, was 'one of the last of the great "stripped classic" palaces which formed the transition between historicism and the Modern Movement' p. 457.

17. Howarth, op. cit., 1977, p. xli.

18. Pevsner, op. cit., 1936, pp. 165–6 and 222.

19. John Betjeman, *First and Last Loves*, London, 1952, p.141. Betjeman, of course, had assisted Morton Shand's campaign in the *Architectural Review* in the 1930s to rediscover designers like Mackintosh, Voysey and Baillie Scott as 'pioneers'.

20. Robert Macleod, *Charles Rennie Mackintosh*, 1968, p. 156.

21. *Journal of the Royal Institute of British Architects*, 1923, p. 513.

22. David Walker, 'The greet modernist of Glasgow' [sic] in the *Times Literary Supplement*, 9 December 1977, p. 1450.

23. Goodhart-Rendel, 1953, op. cit., p. 225.

24. Andor Gomme and David Walker, *Architecture of Glasgow*, 1968, p. 20.

25. Howarth, op. cit., p. 55; David Walker in Robertson (ed.) op. cit., p. 175 etc.

26. The dating of this is slightly obscure. Gomme and Walker reproduce a drawing by Alexander McGibbon which was illustrated in *Academy Architecture* in 1895 and shows both the low banking hall and the block behind with its broken cornices, but before the eaves gallery was added. Incidentally, the recessed, battered, rusticated and curved corners of Burnet's

single-storey banking hall are strikingly similar to those on Behren's celebrated AEG Turbine Hall of 1908.

27. Summerson, 'The British Contemporaries of Frank Lloyd Wright', op. cit.

28. Walker, in the *TLS*, 1977, op. cit.

29. David Walker, 'Scotland and Paris: 1874–1887' in John Frew and David Jones (eds.) *Scotland and Europe: Architecture and Design 1850–1940*, St Andrews Studies in the History of Scottish Architecture and Design, 1991.

30. *The Scots Pictorial*, 29 July 1916, p. 387. Ironically, the year before this anti-German obituary was published, Mackintosh was suspected of being a German spy in Walberswick.

31. Reilly's treatment of Herbert McNair in Liverpool must largely account for Mackintosh's outburst in 'The Chronacle' [sic] of 1927 against 'pompous bounders like a well-known (at least well advertised) professor at Liverpool' published in Alastair Moffat (ed.) *Remembering Charles Rennie Mackintosh*, 1989, pp. 139 and 143. The only mention of Mackintosh in Reilly's autobiography, *Scaffolding in the Sky*, 1938, is as McNair's brother-in-law, 'to whom many give the credit of starting the modern movement in architecture all over the world' (p. 65).

32. Alan Powers, 'Edwardian Architectural Education: a Study of three Schools of Architecture' in *AA files: Annals of the Architectural Association School of Architecture*, no 5, 1984, p. 56.

33. Goodhart-Rendel in *The Architects' Journal*, 27 June 1923, p. 1066.

34. Goodhart-Rendel, 1953, op. cit.

35. Glasgow School of Art Minute Book VI, September 1908, p. 71, quoted in Powers, op. cit., p. 56.

36. Powers, op. cit., p.59.

37. *The Vista*, no 5, Summer 1910, p. 7.

38. *The Vista*, no 4, Autumn 1909, pp. 100–1.

39. *Architectural Review*, May 1913 and June 1914.

40. Both drawings are reproduced in *Academy Architecture*, vol. 41, 1912(i); Burnet subsequently presented one of these to the Royal Academy of Arts as his Diploma Drawing.

41. *The Architects' Journal*, 7 July 1938.

42. Obituary in the *Journal of the Royal Institute of British Architects*, 18 July 1938, p. 895.

SIMON GREEN

William Leiper's Houses in Helensburgh

William Leiper comes from the generation before Mackintosh, but his career overlapped with that of the younger man. He was not only an important Glasgow-based architect, but also, like Mackintosh, a talented artist. He is probably best known for his polychromatic Templeton's Carpet Factory in Glasgow, but his practice was very wide; this chapter looks at a representative sample of his domestic work.

HERMANN Muthesius, in *Das Englische Haus*, recognised William Leiper (1839–1916) as one of 'the leading architects in Scotland today'[1] along with others including Anderson, Blanc and Washington Browne. Unfortunately, information about Leiper's work is scant. His assistant and later partner William Hunter McNab published an overtly adulatory obituary in the *RIBA Journal*,[2] and the *Architectural Record* included an article on him in a series entitled 'Men Who Build'.[3] The contents of his office, which he ran along the lines of a French atelier, were lost in the 1950s.[4]

Leiper had a large and varied practice which covered a wide variety of buildings from a lighthouse on Mull to a polychromatic carpet factory in Glasgow; from a signed tombstone to the interior of the yacht Lividia for the Czar of Russia; from a hospital to the interior of Glasgow City Chambers. In 1900, his design for the Sun Alliance Building in West George Street, Glasgow, won a silver medal in the Paris Exhibition. It is his domestic work, however, which this chapter proposes to discuss, and specifically his work in Helensburgh, where he lived from the age of thirty-seven until his death on 21 May 1916 at the age of seventy-seven.

Leiper was born in 1839, the only child of a mathematics teacher, also William, who ran a school in Renfield Street in Glasgow. He attended the High School of Glasgow, where he must have shown an interest in architecture, for on leaving he entered the successful office of Boucher and Carsland. He then spent a short time in London in the office of W. White and J.L. Pearson, where he was one of the practice's first pupils.[5] During this period, he also met William Burges (1827–81) who, with Pearson, was to sign his RIBA nomination papers. This time in London was to influence his work throughout his career. Before returning to Scotland, he also spent some time in Dublin superintending the erection of Findlater Church for a Mr Heaton.[6] In the early 1860s, he returned to Glasgow, initially to the office of Campbell, Douglas and Sellars, before forming a short-lived partnership with Robert Melvin. Work in this period included Dowanhill Church, Burgh Halls in Partick and Dumbarton and houses in Lanarkshire and

Stirlingshire. In 1871, Leiper gained the commission for a new house for Provost John Ure in Helensburgh. It was probably this large job, coupled with the unfortunate death of his father, that prompted his move with his mother from Glasgow to Helensburgh.

The town founded by the Colquhouns of Luss was a growing resort and, although it had failed as a port, it became a fashionable suburb with good communication links to Glasgow by steamer and train. Leiper always maintained his office in Glasgow, but gained numerous commissions in his adopted home. It is for this reason that Helensburgh is an excellent place to study his diverse domestic work. A broad range of styles was used, and an attempt will be made here to establish stylistic categories in his work.

Cairndhu (Figure 2.1) is the house he built for John Ure in a bold François Premier manner, like a small portion of the great chateau of Chambord transported to the banks of the Clyde. It sits on a prominent site on the western edge of Helensburgh. The policies have been eroded in recent years by executive homes, and the stable block has long since vanished. The plan which Leiper favoured throughout his life is an L-shape with principal rooms in one wing and service rooms in the other. The pale stone exterior hides an extremely rich interior which shows the influence of Japan, which was favoured by the Aesthetic Movement. His only other building to express Anglo-Japanese influence is Castle Park, Biggar. The decorative scheme at Cairndhu, which includes tilework and stained glass, reaches its climax in the drawing room, with its elaborate painted ceiling depicting bamboo, sunflowers and numerous other plants, with an exuberant use of gold (Figure 1.2). Leiper had worked with Daniel Cother, the stained-glass artist, at Dowanhill Church, and his influence is clearly felt here. Leiper's early meeting with Burges affected his approach to interiors, and the contemporary Cornhill House at Biggar for Alexander Kay expresses this Burgessian spirit both internally and externally, where the same massing with dominant corner tower, as at Cairndhu, is clearly expressed.

Around 1872, Leiper built Terpersie, which was to remain his home for the rest of his life. It is a relatively modest house on a suburban feu, but was of sufficient interest to be illustrated by Raffles Davison in the *British Architect*, where it was described thus: 'There is all the Picturesques of picturesque architecture here without the fussiness that goes with so much modern work'.[7] Leiper described the style as 'English Cottage' with deep, overhanging eaves and a dominant chimney stack. It is constructed of yellow sandstone with contrasting red sandstone banding and details. The name derives from Terpersie castle in Aberdeenshire, which Leiper believed to be the ancestral family seat. The castle was a ruin at this time,[8] and tradition has it that Lieper acquired carvings from there which now adorn his Terpersie, including a unicorn and a boar's head. He only appears to have used this style on one further commission, Uplands at Bridge of Allan, which he designed in 1907 as a wedding present from the Sherriff family to their daughter.

The quality of the woodwork and fittings at Terpersie is exceptional, including a

2.1. William Leiper, Cairndhu House, Helensburgh, from the south-east, c. 1871. Built for Provost John Ure. (RCAHMS)

2.2. William Leiper, Cairndhu House, Helensburgh, c. 1871. Detail of Drawing Room ceiling showing Anglo-Japanese decoration inspired by the Aesthetic Movement. (RCAHMS)

stained-glass stair window incorporating his initials, two possibly medieval fragments of portrait busts and the initials MJ. These were previously thought to refer to his housekeeper, but since her name was Catherine McGregor, this attribution seems unlikely. They may be the initials of his mother.

Dalmore originally stood in spacious policies with twin gate lodges on the western edge of the town close to Cairndhu. It was built in 1873–4 for the Bishop family in the 'Old Scots' style. Here, Leiper employed his tremendous knowledge of Baronial architecture to create a truly Scottish building. His numerous paintings and sketching trips provided the inspiration for the rich programme of decoration, including the array of seventeenth-century-inspired dormer heads. The form of the building is taken from Newark Castle at Port Glasgow across the Clyde.[9] Leiper, never being one for wasting a good idea, reused the design a decade later in the Highlands. The house has unfortunately been converted into flats and the policies swamped with housing.

In 1883, Robert Stuart, of Ingliston, near Edinburgh, commissioned Leiper to design a hunting lodge on his newly-acquired estate at the head of Loch Moidart. The plans of Dalmore and Kinlochmoidart are the same, but an extra floor was added in the latter to accommodate the prerequisites of a lodge not required in a seaside villa. The most

35)

fascinating and important fact about Kinlochmoidart is that it has survived unaltered. An album of nineteenth-century photographs in the house shows that the interior survives complete with its furniture, ornaments, pictures and fabrics, although succeeding generations have moved various pieces around. The survival of the house is a testament to the strength and determination of Mrs Nina Stewart, great-granddaughter of the builder. She was advised to demolish everything save the service wing, but has undertaken a colossal programme of restoration and conservation.[10] The house is the most complete example of Leiper's work and affords a glimpse of the richness of his vision.

The house sits on a flat site, sheltered to the north and east by dark hills. The approach, as at Dalmore, affords a view of the garden or west front, with the entrance on the east front. The massing of the building implies that an ancient tower has been extended and modified, but he did not slavishly copy any historic example. It is possible that he built a model of the design, since the masses of the different elements are equally picturesque from every direction, rising from the low servants' wing to the north right up to the housekeeper's erie at the top of the tower. The complex roof structure with its gables, domes and conical turrets provides continuous interest but also, unfortunately, an invitation to water to penetrate among the myriad of valley gutters. It is in this understanding and manipulation of volume that Leiper's expression as an artist is clearly seen. The sculptural programme at Kinlochmoidart includes Leiper's interpretation of Baronial details from as far afield as Castle Girnigoe-Sinclair near Wick, Caithness. A cursory examination of the interior explains why he was such a popular domestic architect. The front door is approached via a wide flight of steps, and the entrance hall runs up another flight before the hall is reached (Figure 2.3). Dark wood dado panelling with rich, dark green flock wallpaper above is lit by intricately leaded windows, one of which is orieled and all of which have different patterns of leadwork. The chimney piece, with its stumpy granite columns and intricate carving, shows the influence yet again of William Burges, as does the stairwell screen. The drawing room originally afforded magnificent views of Loch Moidart from its spacious bay window, and it is the only room to have been redecorated, although the original wallpapers survive beneath a coat of emulsion paint. The adjacent dining room is richly panelled and is of complex shape in which Leiper delights, providing a breakfast room in the round tower, a buffet niche, an ingleneuk fireplace and the remaining rectangle a spacious dining room. The frieze is of Tynecastle canvas, a type of lincrusta developed by William Scott Morton to imitate embossed leather, which became extremely popular. Scott Morton and Leiper met as pupils of Campbell Douglas and remained close friends for life. Scott Morton provided the majority of the furniture throughout the house, including the complete suite of dining-room furniture. The main bedroom on the principal floor was completed with a range of fitted, white-painted furniture of a type more commonly associated with the work of Mackintosh and his circle.

2.3. William Leiper, Kinlochmoidart House, Inverness-shire, 1883, for Mr Robert Stewart. View of hall and stairway showing intricate carving, variety of leaded light work and high-quality woodwork. (RCAHMS)

The lower ground floor is reached by an enclosed stair and contains the rooms required for less formal entertaining: a spacious billiard room; a morning room originally with an adjacent conservatory, now lost; a smoking room; a gun room; and, skilfully incorporated beneath the main entrance steps, a dark room complete with red glass panel incorporated within the shutters. The record that was made by Mr Stewart through his interest in photography has enabled us to realise the full importance of this house. The bedroom floor is reached by a spacious stair lit by a large, arched, leaded window. The landing is a decorative *tour de force*: a rich pattern of greens, blues and golds on an orange ground is created using stencil and wallpapers. This startling scheme survives largely intact and even incorporates the monograms of the owners. One bedroom incorporates a splendid bath within a tiled niche, while all retain their elegant fireplaces. Although a large staff was required to run the house, every modern convenience was installed, including electric light and a refrigeration system, both hydroelectrically-powered and still in working order. A magnificent luggage and log lift survive in the well of the service stair, although this was hand-powered.

Leiper employed the same 'Old Scots' style when he was employed by J.S. Templeton, the carpet manufacturer whose factory he designed in 1889, to extend a mid-nineteenth-century villa at Cove called Knockderry Castle. Templeton was a close friend of Scott Morton, and it is possible that he gained both commissions through this friendship. At Knockderry, he added a tower, with the disabled owner's top-floor bedroom suite reached by a water-powered lift, and a magnificent music hall, originally with an organ and an extensive cycle of paintings which survive.

In 1880, Leiper designed Redholm in Millig Street, Helensburgh, later renamed Wester Millig. This house clearly shows the influence of Pearson's Quar Wood, which was unfortunately radically altered in 1949 but is illustrated in Quincy's book,[11] displaying the same polychromatic slatework cresting and bold modelling. This was not, however, Leiper's first essay in this style; in 1871 he had built Lindsaylands near Biggar, and, as at Dalmore and Kinlochmoidart, Redholm is an exact replica of Lindsaylands, including the same porch and conservatory arrangement. Although they were designed for very different sites and purposes, one a country villa and the other a commuter residence, he was successfully able to convince the clients that this was what they needed.

In the early 1880s, he temporarily gave up architecture to study in Paris, enrolling with, among others, Arthur Melville and Millie Dow at the Studio Julian. He returned to architecture with the unusual commission to design the interior of the royal yacht Lividia for the Czar, then under construction at Elder's shipyard.

In 1883, Leiper built a house on the neighbouring feu to Terpersie. This was a speculative venture, initially called Bonnington and later renamed Rhuarden. It is built in the style of Alexander 'Greek' Thomson, who was a good friend of Leiper's, and MacNab, in the obituary,[12] recalls that Leiper designed various villas in a Thomsonian style; however, as yet this is the only one definitely identified. It has all the features, including a large, semicircular bay window, low-pitched, overhanging eaves and exuberant detailing, that are expected of a 'Greek' Thomson building. In 1901, Leiper added an elegant conservatory.

Brantwoode (Figure 2.4) was designed in 1895 for James Alexander, of the Jameson Oil Refining Company, who was an ardent admirer of Ruskin.[13] The style is influenced by Richard Norman Shaw's half-timbered work exemplified by Cragside, Northumberland. This house provides us with a good, unaltered example of his smaller domestic work with half-timbering, tile-hanging, bargeboard and rich red sandstone combined in an almost painterly manner. The plan, as at Cairndhu, is an L-shape with a library; a living room, incorporating a dining area with serving hatch contrived round a corner to maintain privacy; a parlour with a magnificent corner bay window along the south front, and service quarters in a wing to the north. The living room was designed as a living hall providing the main access to both the parlour and the library. The entrance hall runs to

2.4. William Leiper, Brantwoode House, Helensburgh, 1894, for Mr James Alexander. South elevation showing the large bay window to the right of the parlour and the mixture of materials, half-timbering, slating, stonework and tile-hanging. (RCAHMS)

the north of the principal rooms and contains a fireplace with the quaint motto 'In the world at home, in the home my world'. The entrance is sheltered by an ample porch. Here again, the quality of the interior fittings is extremely high, and all principal rooms have ample ingleneuk fireplaces. The one in the library is decorated with a mosaic panel, and the one in the living room retains a panel of Tynecastle canvas as described at Kinlochmoidart. The windows retain their intricate patterns of leadwork here through-out the principal rooms. Yet again, Leiper reused the design of Brantwoode to create a marine villa for Sir Alexander Walker in 1904 at Piersland, Troon.[14]

Other houses in Helensburgh in this style include Polkemmet, Ardlui and Morar Lodge, this last now called Drumadoon. These houses are all on neighbouring feus to Mackintosh's Hill House. Morar Lodge was built in 1898 and extended by Leiper five years later. It is to the additions we turn, since the 1898 house is of Brantwoode type. Leiper added a new entrance and extended the accommodation into the roof. It is possible that Leiper was influenced by the shingle style, pioneered by Greene and Greene in America, specifically in the dormer window that looks eastwards over Hill House.[15]

2.5. William Leiper, Redtower, Helensburgh, 1900. South front showing the numerous different elements that Leiper was capable of combining successfully in one building. (RCAHMS)

It is not known if Leiper visited America but, in any case, he could have become familiar with the shingle style from the coverage it received in the architectural press.

Another element of the Shaw influence is seen in the extensions carried out to an unexceptional mid-nineteenth-century villa called Clarendon. Here, Leiper added a new wing containing two reception rooms and an entrance hall with porch. The design employs bold Tudor bays such as Shaw used at Adcote, Shropshire, in 1876–81. The quality of the interiors has enabled it to withstand its present use as a school.

Redtower (Figure 2.5) was designed in 1900 and provides another example of Leiper's eclectic taste. Here he combines Shaw-inspired half-timbered gables with a conical-roofed corner tower deriving from the 'Old Scots' of Dalmore. This mixture of stone and half-timbering comes closest to Cragside; however, to them he adds a Scots Renaissance doorpiece which is partnered with boldly balustraded balconies, one supported on substantial scrolled brackets. Yet again, the building, both internally and externally, expresses Leiper's love of materials, of modelling and of massing.

The idea that Leiper was a shy, retiring man has often been quoted.[16] If he was, he did not refrain from leading an extremely active life. He painted throughout his life, being an associate in 1891 and then an elected member of the RSA in 1896. He was the convener of the Haldane Trust of the Glasgow School of Art, and in 1876 was elected the first architect member of the Scottish Arts Club. He was an active member of St Columba's church, being both an office-bearer and a pioneer worker in the Sabbath Morning Meeting.[17] He was a 'Votary of the Wheel'[18] and a keen gardener. He also seems to have maintained an open house at Terpersie for a wide variety of interesting people. He collected contemporary art and was a long-time friend of William MacTaggart, for whom he was best man at the latter's second wedding. He is also reputed to have travelled extensively, although only the trip to Paris in the early 1880s is actually recorded. In addition, there is evidence of a trip to Italy in an illustrated lecture on that subject which he delivered in Helensburgh on 23 January 1894.[19]

It is difficult to summarise the work of such an eclectic architect. Throughout his career, he appears to have been able to provide what the client wanted but also to express his own individuality through his buildings. The term 'Leiperian' was used during his own lifetime, but an exact definition of the term remains elusive. Having said that, it is relatively easy to spot one of Leiper's buildings once one's eye is accustomed to his work. Leiper was not afraid to reuse details and often whole designs if the situation fitted, and his love of colour and movement always brought his designs alive. He was always an artist in whatever medium he worked, and in architecture he managed to tailor his temperament to the different situations that arose to create workable and good-looking houses. Only one area of his work has been dealt with here, but it is one which expresses his versatility very well.

This chapter is based on a paper delivered by Simon Green at the Conference 'Mackintosh and his Successful Contemporaries'.

Royal Commission for the Ancient and Historic Monuments of Scotland

NOTES

1. Hermann Muthesius *Das Englische Haus*, Berlin 1904–5, English translation p. 61.

2. William Hunter MacNab, obituary of Leiper in *RIBA Journal*, 26 August 1916.

3. 'Men who build', *Architectural Record*, 12 January 1898.

4. The contents of the office passed on Leiper's death to William Hunter MacNab, who in his turn bequeathed it to his son William Leiper

MacNab, who died in penury in the 1950s. Information from David
Walker.

5. A. Quincy *John Loughborough Pearson*, Yale 1979, p. 126.

6. Mentioned in the 'Men who build' article (p. 487); see note 3 above.
Mr Heaton has yet to be identified.

7. Raffles Davison in *The British Architect*, 26 January 1883.

8. It has since been lavishly restored, forming a small hotel.

9. W.H. MacNab, op. cit.

10. Carried out by the Edinburgh architects Simpson and Brown.

11. A. Quincy, op. cit., p. 62.

12. W.H. MacNab, op. cit.

13. Brantwoode was named after Ruskin's house in the Lake District,
although curiously mispelt, with an 'e' added at the end.

14. See Mike Davis's article on 'Millionayrshire Mansions' in this *Journal*.

15. I am grateful to Mr David Walker for this observation.

16. Based mainly on the 'Men who build' article and the MacNab
obituary; see notes 2 and 3 above.

17. *Helensburgh and Gareloch Times*, 31 May 1916. Information from Fiona
Sinclair.

18. W.H. MacNab, op. cit.

19. Information from Fiona Sinclair.

20. Davison, op. cit.

A U D R E Y   S L O A N

James Miller: Sixty Years in the History of Scottish Architecture

James Miller, FRIAS, FRIBA, RSA (1860–1947), played an important part in the development of Scottish architecture and yet, in proportion to his long and varied career, surprisingly little has been written about his work. This short study can only serve as a brief introduction to the achievements of this prolific Glasgow architect, whose career spanned sixty years.

THE work of James Miller has been somewhat eclipsed by his contemporaries, possibly due to the rather elusive nature of his work, which is difficult to categorise due to its diversity. The man was capable of handling many styles, using them, where appropriate, in a vast range of projects from 1880 to 1940. Miller did not pretend to be an innovator and, stylistically, he tended to stay a step behind other architects. However, his rather eclectic approach still remains perfectly valid, as it reflects the fickle, changing tastes of society at an important and influential time in the country's history. In addition, Miller's approach sustained a highly successful practice with a constant flow of important commissions from a loyal group of clients.

It was James Miller's early training which established his versatility as an architect. He was born at Auchtergaven in 1860, educated at Perth Academy and, in 1879, started a five-year apprenticeship with Andrew Heiton, a Perth architect who had trained in the office of William Burn and David Bryce and became renowned for his railway work. Heiton's connections with Edinburgh encouraged Miller to work in several offices there, before joining the engineering and architectural department of the Caledonian Railway Company in 1888.

Miller worked for the next five years with the company, designing many stations in the expanding rail network around the country. Miller developed an 'Arts and Crafts'–inspired style for the station buildings, which proved attractive to the travelling public. He also made extensive use of the same style in his domestic buildings from early in his career.

In 1888, Miller won the competition for the Belmont Parish Church in Great George Street, Hillhead, Glasgow (1892–4), which enabled him to start up in a practice of his own,¹ but he continued to work with the Caledonian Railway and its rival companies long after this time. His design for the low-level station at the Botanic Gardens in Glasgow (1893, now demolished; Figure 3.1) reproduced the familiar half-timbering and red brick walls, but it was tinged with an Oriental flavour: it was described at the time as 'a strange sight in Glasgow; it has two tall turrets on the roof with gilded onion-shaped

3.1. James Miller, Botanic Gardens Station, Glasgow, 1893 (now demolished). The picturesque Arts and Crafts style of Miller's early domestic work and station designs is unusually combined with fanciful, exotic detailing which was later developed at the buildings for the 1901 Glasgow International Exhibition. (Mitchell Library)

domes, is very well grouped and detailed, and looks too good architecturally for what it is'.[2] Miller's design for a ticket office in St Enoch Square in 1896, for the Glasgow and District Subway, was also rather whimsical because of its minute scale. This little red sandstone building, crammed with Jacobean detailing, still stands in the square, in defiance of its enormous neighbour, the modern St Enoch Shopping Centre. Even when initially built, Miller's design could not have been anything more than a playful essay, unable to compete with its huge neighbours. Although both this building and the Botanic Garden Station were out of character with their surroundings, they provided good publicity for the companies involved, who at that time were in fierce competition for business and fought to convince the public that their method of transport around the city was the best. Despite this competitive edge, it did not seem to matter that they shared architects, and indeed Miller was employed by all the main companies, who took advantage of his experience in this field of design. This helped him to build up a group of very influential and wealthy clients, and his reputation as an architect grew steadily; it was a reputation greatly enhanced by his skill at winning competitions, and it resulted in an abundance of commissions, large and small, through to the Second World War.

3.2. James Miller, Belfast City Hall, 1897 (competition entry). Miller's design did not win but was one of the three premiated works in the competition and provided the architect with a starting point for the dome of the main pavilion at the 1901 Glasgow International Exhibition. (RIAS Collection)

James Miller's first major competition was for the baroque Municipal Buildings at Clydebank, which were eventually built, after some delay, in 1900. His next competition, considerably greater in scale, was for Belfast City Hall in 1897 (Figure 3.2). Although his design did not win, it was one of the three premiated by the assessor, Alfred Waterhouse, and the 'grouping of the subsidiary masses' in the dome provided Miller with a good starting point for his next major achievement: the 1901 Glasgow International Exhibition.[3]

The 1901 Glasgow International Exhibition in Kelvingrove Park was intended to celebrate the opening of the Glasgow Art Gallery and Museum, which had been built from the profits of the 1888 Exhibition and public subscription.[4] A competition was held which attracted entries from the major Glasgow architects of the day, including Mackintosh, but it was Miller's design which was the favourite: a highly decorative, sixteenth-century Spanish Renaissance style, thought to be 'Far Eastern' by the people of Glasgow but similar to the adjacent Art Gallery and Museum by Simpson and Allen, although more excessive in its fancy detailing and use of colour.[5]

Miller's design for the competition has been heavily criticised over the years. Not only is its taste too sugary for most, but the forty-year-old architect also missed a marvellous opportunity to design his showcase buildings in the latest architectural style, as demonstrated in the art nouveau of the Paris exhibition the year before. Instead, his mood was regressive. With the benefit of hindsight, it would now seem a strange and contradictory image for any vigorous, enterprising and modern city to project to the world in celebration of years of prosperity and as an expression of its optimism for the future. Yet the Exhibition proved to be a great success; its 'Oriental' flavour and romantic, fairytale quality won the hearts of the Edwardians, who were fascinated by lavish and exotic spectacle. The commission enabled him to demonstrate his talents to a wider audience and to become a recognised figure in the architectural profession. He was also elected as an Associate of the Royal Scottish Academy during this year. Miller's practice became well established and, with many other valuable commissions coming in, a bright future was assured.

Miller has been criticised for his rather fickle and eclectic stylistic approach. He dabbled in everything, skilfully changing and reinterpreting styles to suit the individual needs of each client and building-type. His pragmatism was well suited to the nature of society at the turn of the century, when architectural diversification was welcomed. With such a proliferation of new building-types being erected at this time, to improve education, health and living conditions, a broad-minded philosophy almost guaranteed success as an architect.

It is difficult really to capture Miller's thoughts about his work. There is very little evidence about his personal philosophy, and he was not a very public man, as the following quote from his obituary in the RIAS Journal of 1947 demonstrates:

> very reserved by nature, he did not enter much into public life and was well content to let others talk architecture while he was doing the job. Quick-tempered, he could also be very sympathetic and understanding when the occasion demanded. He was also a hard taskmaster, but few of the men who passed through his hands will deny that they benefited to a remarkable degree from being employed by Mr Miller.

Shortly after the Exhibition had ended, there was an article in the *Builder's Journal and Architectural Record* of March 1902, which detailed a lecture James Miller gave to the Architectural Association. In it, Miller admits his respect for engineers, and discusses what he sees as the role of architecture in relation to engineering. As it was reported:

> Mr Miller believes that in their elements architecture and engineering are the same, what difference there is lying in the former adding what may be called the graphic or pictorial element to the latter, harmonizing all parts and appealing to the senses more directly.[6]

The article goes on to highlight the beauty of the unadorned structure of the Exhibition buildings, although 'the pleasure obtained is in proportion to the educated appreciation of the value of these works'. In Miller's opinion, engineers generally neglected to appeal to the needs of the senses, and it was the duty of the architect to 'clothe' the engineering with something more intellectually stimulating and meaningful.

3.3. James Miller, Wemyss Bay Railway Station, 1904. A celebration of pure functional architecture. (RIAS Collection)

And yet it does not take a trained eye to recognise the inherent beauty in the functional engineering to be found in Miller's designs for Wemyss Bay (1904; Figure 3.3) and Stirling (1912–15) railway stations.

Miller's straightforward and practical approach to design did not produce innovative architecture but did provide good-quality solutions in response to a brief and satisfied the demands of public taste, thereby suiting the client and ensuring further commissions.

Following the success of the 1901 Exhibition, projects started to flow in. Miller seemed to be able to work comfortably with an unlimited number of styles, and the next two decades saw a considerable volume of work coming out of the practice. The work from the railway companies began to diversify, and quite often the results showed American influences, as in the facades of the large hotels like Turnberry (1904), the extension to Peebles Hydro (1904) and the extension to Sir Rowand Anderson's Central Station Hotel in Hope Street, Glasgow (1906), with the beautifully curving elevations to the station concourse. His commercial and public buildings were neo-Baroque, as exemplified in his offices for the Caledonian Railway Company in Union Street, Glasgow, also in the recently refurbished Classic cinema in Renfield Street, Glasgow (1914–16) and the Institute of Civil Engineers in London (1910). Other work included the interior of the The Lusitania (1907); many mansions and houses, such as Kildonan Mansion,

3.4. James Miller, Union Bank of Scotland, St Vincent Street/Renfield Street, Glasgow, 1924. A typical example of the American-inspired commercial buildings produced by Miller's practice during the Twenties when Richard Gunn was the chief draughtsman. (RIAS Collection)

3.5. James Miller, Commercial Bank of Scotland, West George Street/West Nile Street, Glasgow, 1930. Compared to earlier commercial work, decoration in the white Portland stone is minimal, highlighting aspects of the modernism which Miller continued to develop throughout the 1930s, particularly in his hospital buildings. (RIAS Collection)

Barrhill (1915); churches such as the picturesque art nouveau St Andrew East Church, Alexandra Parade, Glasgow (1904); and the neo-Jacobean Natural Philosophy building for the University of Glasgow (1905).

The American influence evident in some of his prewar work was even more marked in Miller's commercial work of the 1920s due to the assistance of Richard Gunn, Miller's chief draughtsman and designer, who joined the firm in 1918. The Union Bank of Scotland headquarters in Renfield Street (Figure 3.4) is a superb specimen, drawing its inspiration directly from York and Sawyer's Guaranty Trust building, New York. This was pictured in the Architectural Review USA in 1913, a copy of which was lent to Gunn before the competition for the bank in 1924.[7] A beautiful presentation drawing for this building was submitted to the RSA during the year of his election there in 1930. Other examples of this type of work in Glasgow can be found in the McLaren Warehouse on the corner of George Square and Hanover Street (1923), the Prudential Assurance Building, Renfield Street (1928) and the two Portland stone banks in Bothwell Street (1934) and West George Street (1930) for the Royal Bank of Scotland (Figure 3.5).

Around the time of Gunn's death in 1933, there was a distinct change of approach in Miller's practice. The brick neo-Georgian was initially favoured, and was used in several municipal buildings such as Troon (1930) and Stirling (1931), his home town. Gradually, a pure white, streamlined modernism developed for the late hospital work, as at Canniesburn (1935) and Larbert Colony (1934). James Miller was encouraged to retire by the RIAS at the age of eighty so that he could receive an Honorary Fellowship in recognition of sixty years in the profession, and the practice was taken over by one of his assistants, John Wellwood Manson.

James Miller's work is not simply of passing interest within the context of Scottish architectural history. It is of relevance that Miller was a direct contemporary of Charles Rennie Mackintosh and, in the 1901 competition for the Exhibition, succeeded where Mackintosh failed. Although it is without doubt that Mackintosh was the superior designer, as were some of the other men around at this time, Miller was an able and accomplished architect, with a pragmatic approach which led to a long and successful career, and for this reason his work cannot be overlooked. It is hoped that this brief overview of James Miller's career will contribute a little to a greater understanding of the architecture produced in Glasgow during the famous Mackintosh era and perhaps provoke debate about the definition of success in the architectural world.

Audrey Sloan was a student at the Mackintosh School of Architecture until 1991

NOTES
1. 'Men You Know—No 1487', *The Bailie*, 17 April 1901, p. 1
2. *Builder*, 9 July 1898.
3. *Builder's Journal and Architectural Record*, xv, 1902, p. 54.

4. P. Kinchin and J. Kinchin, *Glasgow's Great Exhibitions*, Bicester, 1988, p. 55.

5. Ibid., p. 60.

6. *Builder's Journal and Architectural Record*, xv, 1902, p. 54.

7. A. Gomme and D. Walker, *Architecture of Glasgow*, London, 1987, p. 270.

A Profile of Sir George Washington Browne

Our perception of the architectural scene in Scotland around the turn of the
twentieth century is distorted by an absence of monographs on many of its
leading protagonists. One of the giants requiring evaluation is the subject
of this chapter, which will touch the surface of this shortfall (Figure 4.1).
His former assistant, John Wilson, reported in his obituary that 'Sir
Rowand Anderson, Sir George Washington Browne, Sir John Burnet, Mr
Hippolyte J. Blanc and John Kinross, these were big men to all of us in the
days of our architectural adolescence.'[1] This brief introduction to Browne is
an attempt to identify his major achievements, drawing on widely diverse
primary and secondary material in the absence of an official archive.[2] His
place in the wider context will be suggested by the other chapters in this
volume.

BORN in Glasgow in 1853, Browne did not come from a particularly wealthy background: his father worked for Glasgow Corporation Gas
Company.[3] He began his architectural apprenticeship in the office of Salmon, Son and
Ritchie in Glasgow in about 1870 where he remained until 1873, studying simultaneously
at Glasgow School of Art.[4] He then joined the influential practice of Campbell Douglas
and Sellars, either as draughtsman or to complete his apprenticeship. His skills of
draughtsmanship first received public recognition in 1874 when he won the John James
Stevenson prize for measured drawings.[5] Stevenson had previously partnered Campbell
Douglas in Glasgow before moving to London, where he maintained strong links with
his former city and its offspring. The calibre of Browne's educational foundation was
taken further when he moved to this London office, then Stevenson and Robson, in
1875.[6] Here he remained for a further two years before joining Sir Arthur W. Blomfield
as assistant in 1877, and then William Eden Nesfield, presumably in the same capacity.
These London years, passed in the offices of leading contemporary architects, furnished
Browne with invaluable experience and insight into the profession.

In 1877, he won the most important prize of his life, the Pugin Travelling Studentship,
which enabled him to travel in Britain, sketching subjects which he subsequently
compiled into a publication in 1887. He declared in the Preface to the *Pugin Studentship
Drawings*:

> The author is not without hope that these gleanings from his student work
> may contribute a little towards fostering that interest in and regard for
> our venerable architectural remains.

4.1. Sir George Washington Browne, in his prime, circa 1901, at the home which he designed, The Limes, Blackford Road, Edinburgh (photograph taken from the *Souvenir Programme of the Opening of Bo'ness Town Hall and Carnegie Library*, of which he was the architect). (RCAHMS)

This hope was admirable in itself, but we may presume that in addition his publication was intended 'to encourage and promote the study of old work as the best possible means of acquiring the knowledge necessary to design good new work', the intention which lay behind the Stevenson prize.[7] The published drawings contained medieval, ecclesiastic and later domestic subjects; they served as an entrée to leading patrons of the day and established for him a place among scholarly architects.

He moved to the Edinburgh office of Robert Rowand Anderson in 1879 as principal assistant, and was to remain in the city for the rest of his career. A Glasgow and London training provided a most unusual foundation for an Edinburgh architect, and accounted for his fresh, widely-informed approach. In 1881, he joined Anderson in partnership as Anderson and Browne, forming one of the most influential practices on the east coast of Scotland. He had arrived at a critical point in Anderson's career, and encouraged him to bolder design. They were joined in 1883 by Hew Montgomerie Wardrop as Wardrop,

Anderson and Browne. Most notable among their work in these years were the feuing and terrace designs on the Braid Estate, Morningside, Edinburgh, where Browne's London experience clearly bore fruit.[8] Here, the Queen Anne style, securely rooted in England, was transported to Scotland in stone in their designs for Nile Grove and Hermitage Terrace, 1881–4, demonstrating the intimate, feminine scale synonymous with the free classic style. The significance of this introduction should not be underestimated: it sparked the search for a traditional indigenous style in response to the comfort, convenience and requirements of contemporary life. Sydney Mitchell, A.N. Paterson, Hippolyte Blanc, John Kinross and others took up the challenge. The Braid Estate designs indicate how considerable was the influence of Stevenson, the author of *House Architecture* (1880), and of Nesfield, on the young architect, and his influence in turn on Anderson. The Braid Estate echoed the artistic suburb of Bedford Park in London. Shavian influences were brought to Scotland by Browne in other building-types, notably the mansion flats at Bruntsfield Place, Edinburgh, 1887–8. In Queen Anne garb, gentle in design but assured, these provide a forward-looking approach to the traditional tenement. They comprise an asymmetrical composition, breaking away from the common formula of repetitive units.

Browne joined the contemporary search for a Scottish variant of Queene Anne, translating the principles of commodity, convenience and reduced scale to an indigenous style, and this may be seen most clearly in the Scottish seventeenth-century style chosen for Langlees, near Biggar, 1891. However, he retained an admiration for the Old English work of Shaw and Nesfield, and his Cossar Ewart House, Penicuik (now the Craigie House Hotel), 1885–9, and Martin Hardie House and Studio (the Drumsheugh Toll), Belford Road, Edinburgh, 1891, fulfilled the same goals but were derivative of English sources. Hints of Sussex vernacular, including half-timbering, pargetting and a Shavian ingleneuk, were included in the Penicuik house, while arty details such as stamped plasterwork adorned the Belford Road house.

Blomfield's fine Gothic churches no doubt impressed Browne and provided him with the confidence to adopt an avant garde approach for his Morningside Braid Church in 1886. He chose a unique, baptistery-like, octagonal form and showed an Italian Renaissance love of colour (originally shown in marbled sections of the exterior). Strong reference was made here to the church designs by James Sellars.[9] Such a centrally-planned church with galleried interior was a reversion in contemporary ecclesiastic design in Edinburgh, and its orientation on the site was excellent. The only other complete church design by Browne was the imposing Maisondieu Church in Brechin, 1891, where he employed a late classic style with Greek detailing, again drawing on Glasgow precedents for certain details, notably the use of Greek Ionic. He carried out several interior refurbishments of churches, notably at the Apostolic Church in Davie Street, 1886, and Lady Glenorchy's Church, Greenfield Place, 1893, in Edinburgh. He designed several church halls (and several public halls), for example at Eyre Crescent, Edinburgh (now demolished), and a number of organ cases, such as the impressive classical designs for the Palmerston Place and Broughton Place Churches in Edinburgh.

Neither domestic nor ecclesiastic architecture would become Browne's leading field, but his contributions to both were significant. He made his mark primarily in public, commercial and institutional commissions. In 1885, he left Wardrop and Anderson, on friendly terms, and began independent practice, seeking perhaps to leave the Gothic-inspired design world of Anderson to which he had contributed Early Renaissance expertise (see Anderson's Medical School and McEwan Hall, Edinburgh), and to enjoy greater freedom of expression and recognition. David Walker considers that the formation of a triple partnership in 1883, with Hew Montgomerie Wardrop, may inadvertently have necessitated Browne's departure, there being insufficient work for the three partners.

A major landmark in Browne's career came with his success in the competition for Edinburgh's Public Library, the first Carnegie Library in Scotland, in 1887 (Figure 4.2). His mastery of the functional requirements and practicalities of library design led to a host of commissions across Scotland and his authorship of a slim history and advisory booklet, *The Planning of Public Libraries*.[10] The choice of the François Premier style and dexterity with its vocabulary, combined with the successful planning, places the library among Browne's outstanding achievements. The sources of inspiration for this style were manifold, not least Browne's travels in Paris, the time he spent with Nesfield, the number of recent publications on French architecture, and the arrival in the office of the Beaux-Arts-trained assistant, Stewart Henbest Capper.[11] Wilson tells, in his obituary on Browne, that his admiration for French Renaissance replaced the former favourite, the Gothic styles. Greek-cross in plan, the library extends down four storeys to the Cowgate, a descent mirrored in his later, five-storey extension to the Advocate's Library across the road.[12] Other impressive library designs by Browne may be found in Bo'ness, Kelso and Annan. He used the François Premier style again in his design for the British Linen Bank, 69 George Street, Edinburgh (now the Bank of Scotland), an unusual choice among the palazzo-like and Classical styles which prevailed for such buildings.

Browne had established a firm foothold in the architectural circles of Edinburgh by 1887. He was a shrewd man, with a fiery temper, a commanding presence, courtly manners and strong convictions.[13] His involvement with the Edinburgh Architectural Association was considerable, continuing his earlier participation with the Glasgow Architectural Association.[14] He served as President of the society between 1883 and 1886, a role also filled by Thomas Ross, David MacGibbon and Blanc. The admirable programme of events and lectures, sketchbook publications and the excellent library facility illustrate the

4.2. Sir George Washington Browne, The Edinburgh Public (Carnegie) Library, George IV Bridge, Edinburgh, 1887. This perspective drawing was exhibited at the Royal Scottish Academy in 1888. The choice of François Premier style was innovative and indicative of the architect's love of the French Renaissance. He used the style again for the bank at 69 George Street, Edinburgh, 1905. (RCAHMS)

academic bias of the group and their strong hold on the patronage of the Edinburgh élite.[15]

Commercial designs were given a unique distinction at Browne's hand, and two in particular form a related pair: the department store, Messrs Redfern Premises (Figure 4.3). 31–32 Princes Street, Edinburgh, 1891 (now demolished), and Mrs Cranston's Tea Rooms, 91 Buchanan Street, Glasgow, 1896 (now the Clydesdale Bank). The banded masonry of each was designed to temper the verticality of elevation imposed by their sites. Messrs Redfern was composed with Gothic detailing with Germanic cupola, while Mrs Cranston's property was given the Northern Renaissance, 'Pont Street Dutch' style. Brown's treatment of the restrictions of the narrow sites echoed designs by English contemporaries, as illustrated in *The Builder* and contemporary periodicals. The bold arches which characterise the designs quickly became a trademark of the architect. The interiors of both properties were excellent: those at Messrs Redfern were featured in

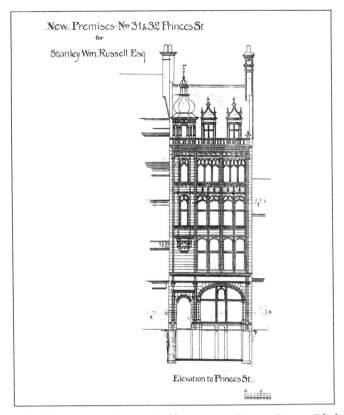

New Premises N° 31 & 32 Princes St
for
Stanley Wm. Russell Esq

Elevation to Princes St.

4.3 Sir George Washington Browne, Messrs Redfern, 31–32 Princes Street, Edinburgh, 1891 (now demolished). This decorative building found a companion piece in Browne's Northern Renaissance design for Mrs Cranston's Tea Rooms at 91 Buchanan Street, Glasgow. Both responded to the constraints of a narrow site with similarly articulated elevations realised in different styles. (Edinburgh City Archives, Dean of Guild Drawings)

Academy Architecture in 1894, and those at the tea rooms, by Charles Rennie Mackintosh and George Walton, were praised by Sir Edwin Lutyens.[16]

The masterful Jacobean design of Browne's Royal Hospital for Sick Children, Sciennes Road, Edinburgh, 1892, demonstrates an earlier use of the English Renaissance. He submitted a magnificent bird's-eye perspective of the hospital as his RSA Diploma drawing. The symmetrical composition, realised in warm Corsehill sandstone with contrasting slates, answered a plan carefully tailored to the specialised demands of a busy hospital. It was a masterpiece and confirmed Browne's place as leader of the younger generation of architects on the east coast of Scotland, fulfilling the same role as the younger J.J. Burnet in the west.

After such immediate success with the Jacobean style, it was not surprising that it was chosen as appropriate for the various subsequent branches of the British Linen Bank, produced in partnership with John More Dick Peddie (1853–1921). Peddie and Browne began their joint practice in the mid-1890s after the death of Peddie's former partner, Charles Kinnear, in 1894, and continued periodically until about 1910, both also producing independent designs from about 1905, while continuing to share the same address, 8 Albyn Place. Many of the designs produced by the joint practice (not least the British Linen Banks) are stylistically related to works carried out by Browne prior to its formation, and we can assume that Peddie's contribution to the firm's designs was secondary to that of Browne, and that, where it occurred, it was more academic and constrained than that of his partner. Bank designs were provided in Linlithgow, Renfrew, Forfar, Crieff, Annan, Melrose, Falkirk, Alloa, Grangemouth and elsewhere. The grandeur of the Royal Bank Offices designed by the practice for Dundee High Street, circa 1898, provided a foretaste of Edwardian classicism, and as such would have stood more comfortably in the streetscapes of Glasgow or London. A varient of this palazzo-like design was used shortly afterwards for the Dublin Insurance Company's building.

Further notable works by the partnership include the Jacobean Scottish Equitable building in St Andrew Square, Edinburgh, 1899, blended with French Renaissance details. The Caledonian Hotel, Edinburgh, 1898–1902, shows a mastery of eclectic design, artfully incorporating the Kinnear and Peddie station buildings, while subtly updating their original detailing in the new section of Corinthian columned arcading, and respectful of the converging terminal vistas at the west end of Princes Street.

Lacking influential connections, unlike Anderson or Wardrop, Browne was compelled to enter competitions and seek commissions, exertions which won him several key projects (not least the Edinburgh Public Library and the King Edward VII Memorial Gates at Holyrood). However, several fine designs by him were submitted unsuccessfully in competition. He entered drawings for the Glasgow Municipal Buildings, for Stirling Station in partnership with Peddie (Figure 4.4), the London County Council Buildings, the Welsh National Monument and the Usher Hall.[17] While he won the competition for the bridge opposite St Paul's in London, it was never executed, the project destroyed by the First World War.

It must be recognised that, in his later career, Browne's style changed. He departed from the free, asymmetrical composition of his youth, producing more formal, conservative designs such as the Edwardian Renaissance YMCA, South St Andrew Street, Edinburgh, 1914–15. His original designs for the King Edward VII Memorial gates were similarly more academic in concept.

Browne saw architecture as an art first and a profession second. He fought with other architects for associateship status of the RSA in 1892 and became a full academician in 1902. He was an active member throughout his career, working closely with John Kinross, serving as Treasurer from 1917 and President from 1924 to 1933 (the first architect president). He was knighted for his services to architecture in 1926, the year of the RSA centenary exhibition. He bemoaned the general indifference to modern architecture in an article in the *Scottish Art Review*, noting that people did not linger in the streets to look at buildings as they would in an art gallery to study paintings: he concluded that 'the absence of a personal identity of the architect with his work has much to do with the lack of interest in this important department of art'.[18] Certainly, his works bear a distinction which defies anonymity, and we can appreciate what he was striving to achieve.

There was much sadness in the architect's life: he was twice married, and his three sons predeceased him, killed during the war or from its effects. He died at his daughter's home in Sambrook, Shropshire, on 15 June 1939, aged eighty-six. Unlike several of his contemporaries, Browne remained active in his profession until the end, if not as a practising architect, then as an assessor in competitions. He confronted the changed architectural stage after the war with vigour rather than shunning its economical constraints and new legislation, submitting designs to the RSA offering solutions to the problem of corner sites and flatted housing, and he expressed a keen interest in local authority housing. He was appointed to the newly-instituted Royal Fine Art Commission in 1927, where his single most significant contribution lay in his influential comments on the St Andrew's House design.[19]

At a time when architectural education was being formalised, Browne took the opportunity to raise the standards of design, working through the RSA Board of Management, and serving as Head of the Architecture Section at Edinburgh College of Art after Rowand Anderson. His pupils included Norman Dick of Glasgow. He was opposed to Modern Movement designs, scorning 'the originality which has no origin', remaining true to his studious, historicist education and showing no interest in contemporary American design, unlike his west-coast colleagues.[20] His exceptional draughtsmanship delighted the members of his practice, who would, apparently, take pains to see the masterpiece currently on his drawing-board.

Among the many war memorials which left Brown's office in the aftermath of the First World War was an imaginative but unexecuted scheme for a Scottish national momument on Calton Hill (Figure 4.5).[21] It was not intended to rival Lorimer's design for the Castle, nor to complete the Parthenon, but rather to enable the sister arts to combine in a triumphal requiem on this appropriate and prominent site.

Sir George Washington Browne captained a small group of Edinburgh-based architects between 1880 and 1914 who together injected a refreshing vitality, while yet providing stability, to a rapidly-changing architectural scene. They steered architecture out of the doldrums of the preceding decades into a more fruitful period. Browne was an architect of excellence, not only in elevation: he was a master of specialised planning, from libraries to hospitals, and handled awkward sites with ingenious savoir-faire. His

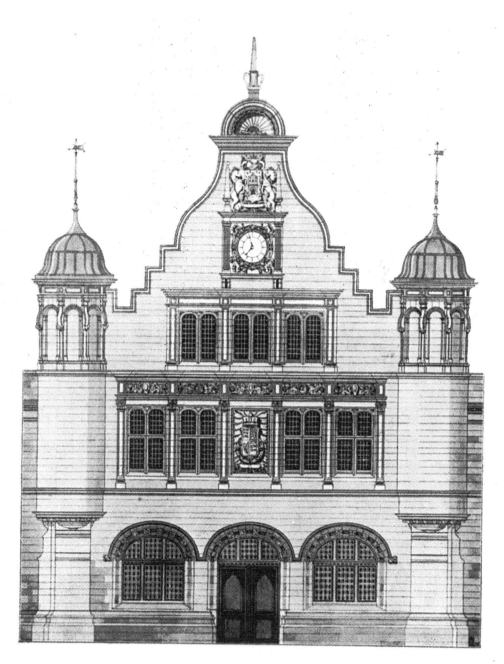

754. *Stirling Station Buildings, Study for Façade*,
PEDDIE AND WASHINGTON BROWNE, R.S.A., Architects.

4.5 Sir George Washington Browne, Suggestion for Completion of the National Monument, Calton Hill, Edinburgh as a War Memorial, 1918, taken from a slim publication by that name. Browne's design was not intended to compete with Sir Robert Lorimer's memorial at the Castle, but rather to complement it. (RCAHMS)

command of revival styles was warmly received, even in Edinburgh, the most conservative of capital cities, and to his credit lie a wealth of fine public and commercial designs, works of art in themselves, scattered around the urban landscapes of Scotland.

This chapter is based on a paper delivered by Deborah Mays at the conference 'Mackintosh and his Successful Contemporaries'.

Historic Scotland

4.4 Peddie and Washington Browne, Stirling Station Buildings, Study for Facade, 1902 (unexecuted). Several trademarks of the partnership are readily apparent in the elements and style of the well-balanced design and may be seen in many of their British Linen Banks across Scotland. James Miller's design for the station was adopted in 1913. (*Academy Architecture*, 1902 i)

ACKNOWLEDGEMENTS

My heartfelt thanks to David Walker for his guidance and helpful comments during my researches and during the composition of this chapter.

NOTES

1. John Wilson, from his obituary on Browne, *Quarterly of the Incorporation of Architects in Scotland*, 1939, pp. 12–13.

2. The major obituaries on Browne are repetitive but contain useful information: see Wilson, cited above; *The Builder*, 23 June 1939; *Scotsman*, 16 June 1939; *Architect and Building News*, 23 June 1939; *RSA Annual Report*, 1939; *RIBA Journal*, 17 July 1939.

3. This minimal information on Browne's father was gained from his Confirmation and Inventory at the SRO, SC.70/1/1027 and SC.70/4/757. He left a surprisingly small estate to the value of £1,930.

4. See George Shaw Aitken *History and Reminiscences of the Edinburgh Architectural Association* (1913) pp. 65–7. Further information on Browne's training may be found in his RIBA statement for nomination, 24 May 1926.

5. *Glasgow Herald*, 25 December 1874, p. 5.

6. J.J. Stevenson and E.R. Robson produced many fine and distinctive Board School designs.

7. *Glasgow Herald*, 25 December 1874, p. 5. Nesfield's example in publishing *Specimens of Medieval Architecture* will also have convinced Browne of the advisability of pursuing such a course.

8. See R.M.H. Forster *Sir Robert Rowand Anderson and his Partnership with Sir George Washington Browne*, Edinburgh University, 1976, for a more detailed examination of the joint practice.

9. David Walker identified the link between the Morningside Braid Church and the work of James Sellars, notably the unexecuted design featured in John Keppie's Memoirs in the *Scottish Art Review* (1888). He also notes that the Maisondieu Church, Brechin, referred to below, made stylistic reference to the works by Sellars and Burnet, not only in use of the Greek Order, but also in the Beaux-Arts mullion and transom cross windows.

10. This monograph was formed from a paper read to the Architectural Section of the Philosophical Society of Glasgow, first printed in *The Builder*. It is thirty-nine pages long, with no illustrations and no date.

11. Browne mentions his continental travels in Paris and Belgium in his RIBA statement (cited above in note 4). Robert Naismith, in *The Scotsman* 'Dash of Genius on City Skyline', 23 Decemeber 1991, gives brief details of Henbest Capper's movements.

12. For details of the protracted birth of the Advocate's Library extension and its notable fitness to purpose, see Iain Gordon Brown *Building for Books: the Architectural Evolution of the Advocate's Library 1689–1925*, 1989, pp. 212–22.

13. John Blythe Kinross CBE, the son of Browne's close friend John Kinross, reported on Browne's character. The obituaries cited in notes 1 and 2 above give further information.

14. See GAA Sketchbook volume III, 1888, drawings of Kent subjects by Browne.

15. The EAA archive and editions of the sketchbooks are kept at the National Monuments Record of Scotland.

16. Perilla Kinchin *Tea and Taste: the Glasgow Tea Rooms 1875–1915*, 1991, pp. 50–2, and pp. 85–91. Lutyens's comments are extracted from C. Percy and J. Ridley (eds) *The Letters of Edwin Lutyens to his Wife Lady Emily*, 1985, p. 49f. and pp. 56–7.

17. The RSA Library holds drawings by Browne for the LCC buildings, the St Paul's Bridge and various other commissions, together with several photographs probably retained from RSA exhibitions.

18. *Scottish Art Review*, 1888–9, pp. 57–9. Written in response to John Honeyman's article 'On the Exhibiting of Architectural Drawings'.

19. David M. Walker, *St Andrews House: an Edinburgh Controversy 1912–1939*, Edinburgh, 1989.

20. J. Wilson, obituary on Browne, RIAS Quarterly, 1939, p. 13.

21. George Washington Browne, slim, illustrated brochure entitled *Suggestion for Completion of the Scottish National Monument, Calton Hill as a War Memorial*, Edinburgh; no date.

Lorimer's Castle Restorations

*This chapter aims to demonstrate the importance of Professor James
Lorimer's restoration of Kellie Castle and the castle restorations carried out
by his son, Robert. It also gives a brief context for such restoration work in
the mid- to late nineteenth century.*

IN ANY consideration of Mackintosh's successful contemporaries,
the name of Sir Robert Lorimer must spring most readily to mind as the Scottish architect
who achieved comparable popular recognition both here and on the Continent. This
popularity has been sustained both by the ease of access to many of his major works in
Scotland, such as the Thistle Chapel and Hill of Tarvit House, and by Peter Savage's
profusely-illustrated book published in 1980, *Lorimer and the Edinburgh Craft Designers.*[1]

One of the most engaging aspects of Lorimer's work is his approach to restoration and
its reflection of the earlier restoration of Kellie Castle carried out by his father. Kellie
had been steadily decaying through the earlier nineteenth century when James Lorimer
and his family stumbled across it on a walk from Pittenweem where they were spending
the summer holidays. Later, the Lorimers acquired a lease on the castle and Professor
Lorimer undertook a remarkably sensitive restoration of the building.

The restoration debate had already begun by the time that James Wyatt was employed
to restore Salisbury Cathedral in 1789. It was the restoration of ecclesiastical buildings
which remained central to this debate and on which passions ran high: 'All that is vile,
cunning and rascally is included in the term Wyatt' was Pugin's familiar condemnation
of the work at Salisbury Cathedral.[2] By the mid-nineteenth century, attention was being
directed to ancient monuments, as well as churches, with Sir George Gilbert Scott's call
for the preservation of the nation's ruins in 1862.[3]

In Scotland, a renewed interest in domestic architecture of the fifteenth and sixteenth
centuries was evinced by the publication of Robert Billings's *Baronial and Ecclesiastical
Antiquities of Scotland* in 1848–52. Billings set himself apart from the previous chroniclers
of Scottish antiquities, such as Grose, claiming greater archaeological exactitude and
criticising the earlier romantic images of ivy-clad ruins.[4] 'Constant has been the watch
against fancy, either on the part of the delineator or the engraver', he boasted, in the
introduction to the first volume.[5]

However, the *Baronial and Ecclesiastical Antiquities of Scotland* had been produced for
the architect William Burn, neatly furnishing him with a pattern book of 'accurate
representations of interesting details'[6] with which to revive the national style. Burn,

Bryce and their contemporaries had a flexible attitude to restoration as applied to the Baronial castles from which they drew their inspiration. Their interpretation of the term 'restoration' often extended to doubling the size of the original dwelling, which was, at times, only retained as the dominant element in a greater scheme. Their interior restorations were often carried out on similar principles, At Thirlestane Castle, Burn and Bryce were commissioned to carry out internal refurbishment. The intention had been to preserve as much of the original work as possible, but in the event all but the principal rooms were completely renewed. Similarly, at Brodie Castle, Morayshire, Burn's admiration of Baronial details did not stop short of mock wood-graining a white, enriched plaster ceiling.

The giants at the centre of the restoration debate in the second half of the nineteenth century were John Ruskin and William Morris. In 1849, the *Seven Lamps of Architecture*, Ruskin introduced a new attitude to antiquities by suggesting that 'the greatest glory of a building is in its age'.[7] He also proposed the idea that at the root of restoration was forgery and deception; 'the more exact the imitation the more it is adapted to mislead posterity'.[8] This was the antithesis of the then current belief that a new copy was of as great value as the original. Ruskin's writing fired the imagination of a new generation of architects and patrons alike.

In March 1877, William Morris founded his 'anti-scrape' society, the Society for the Protection of Ancient Buildings (SPAB). From restoration work characterised by reconstruction and remodelling, the new generation took preservation as their watchword, introducing a regard for protection and conservation. Morris echoed Ruskin's impassioned championing of antiquity. In 1849, Ruskin had preached that, as regards old buildings, 'we have no right whatever to touch them. They are not ours. They belong partly to those who built them and partly to all generations of mankind who are to follow us.'[9] In 1877, Morris called for their preservation because they 'are not in any sense our property, to do as we like with, we are only trustees for those who come after us'.[10] At the same time, there was a greater understanding and appreciation of old building techniques. Billings writes of the use of local materials and the 'ingenuity of the workman's hammer'.[11] The culminating achievement came with the publication of David Macgibbon and Thomas Ross's *Castellated and Domestic Architecture of Scotland*, issued in five volumes from 1887 to 1892. This also broke new ground by including examples of burgh architecture.

The picture which emerges is of a growing awareness and appreciation of an ecclesiastical heritage and later of the different categories of domestic architecture. In Scotland, the Baronial castles of the fifteenth and sixteenth centuries were being considered in a new academic light by the middle of the nineteenth century.

In 1878, Professor James Lorimer began the restoration of Kellie Castle and set about carefully researching its history. His research was collected into a handwritten volume bound in red leather, known as the 'Red Book of Kellie'. Macgibbon and Ross used this volume when they came to write their description of the Castle in *Castellated and Domestic Architecture of Scotland*.[12] The 'Red Book' is fundamental to an understanding of the restoration of Kellie which Professor Lorimer undertook. It illustrates the high level of responsibility he accepted and the amount of research and commitment which he dedicated, over a sustained period of time, to the satisfactory preservation of a threatened ruin. It is remarkable that, in the course of Professor Lorimer's restoration, only minor elements were changed externally and the only additions were the stables and servants' accommodation to the east.

In 1829, after a succession of childless owners, the castle, lands and title of Earl of Kellie passed to the Earl of Mar. The end of the 'Red Book' describes how little attention was paid to Kellie by its owners after the death of the seventh Earl in 1797. After the death of Sir Methven Erskine in 1829, the contents of the house were dispersed and the castle and grounds were neglected. The small farm was let, and the tenant apparently rooted out the shrubs and ploughed up the approach to the castle. For a short time, the manager of a coal pit made a temporary home in the great hall. By the time the Lorimers arrived, the roof had given way in many places.

The condition of the castle when its rehabilitation was taken on has always been described as ruinous. The 'Red Book' gives the fullest description of the dilapidated state of the castle:

> Piles of sticks from birds' nests which, having fallen down the chimneys, reached far into the rooms, every pane of glass had been broken and swallows or house martins built nests in the coronets of the ceilings. The ceilings themselves dipped and in some places had fallen in. Dandelions, grass, and nettles grew in the rooms, and trees had rooted themselves in the walls, where large cracks rapidly extended. The garden wall largely survived but the garden was overgrown with neglected gooseberry bushes, gnarled apple trees and old-world red and white roses.[13]

An early photograph published in 1866 of the north facade of Kellie shows that the main structure was in reasonable repair.[14] The walls had been preserved by the harling which can be seen patchily over the wall surface, gradually being pushed away from the wall by the damp left unchecked for two generations. Janet Alice Lorimer wrote describing the scene:

> The upper windows were all boarded up and in those of the front of the house not one pane remained unbroken. This accounted for the tons of road metal which covered the floors of the rooms. The old road had ceased to exist, a cart track led up the side of the ploughed field, which in its turn was carried right up to the walls of the castle. The present gravelled court-yard or recess being given over to nettles and the paving stones, of which only a few remain, were covered by earth and weeds. The old garden had become a cail yard. The beech tree which was

brought down in 1880 still stood. The old oak window frames were found to be perfectly sound so that the re-glazing of them was not a very serious business and the other assistance given by Lord Kellie was confined to repairing the roof, which he did not, however, do in the most thorough or substantial manner.[15]

The Kellie Castle estate was entailed, preventing Professor Lorimer from feuing it, as he originally wished, and limiting the length of time for which a lease could be drawn up. Permanency of the let was one of the major considerations in order to justify spending so much time and energy on effecting the restoration. Several drafts were made of the lease before Professor Lorimer was satisfied. In the correspondence between Lorimer and the Earl's lawyers, we are given an essential insight into Lorimer's criteria for restoring the castle. In one of the final letters from Professor Lorimer, he states:

> I certainly should hope not only to preserve this beautiful monument of antiquity and its surroundings in decent repair but to cherish and adorn them. But this I must be permitted to do in accordance with my own taste and in relation to my circumstances; and if I am to go to Kellie Castle at all, I must positively decline to place myself in the power of anyone as to what operations I shall execute on the house and grounds. I am willing to promise that in my hands the castle shall retain the general external aspect which it at present presents, but beyond this I will promise nothing.[16]

The final agreement reached stipulated that the Earl of Mar and Kellie should spend £200 in repairs and alterations and that the rent would be £25 per annum. The castle was to be insured for £1,500 and the Lorimers were to spend £600 in building a servant's house, coach house and stable and in improving and repairing the castle. The satisfactory nature of the final lease for the Lorimers is not so surprising when one remembers that James Lorimer was Professor of Public Law at Edinburgh University.

The work of restoration was carried out by a local architect from Elie, John Currie, whose principal talent would seem to have been the ability to gather round him excellent craftsmen. The *East of Fife Record* described the extent of the work:

> The stone stairs which lead to the upper chambers of the castle have been carefully repaired and one of the rooms in the north-west tower has been fitted up as a studio for Mr John Henry Lorimer, . . . The drawing room, formerly used as the banqueting room, is about 49 feet long, and is elegantly furnished. Adjoining is the Professor's study, . . . In one of the rooms the work on the ceiling, done by an Italian and similar to what can be seen in Balcaskie House, is considered the finest in Fife, and the portion partially destroyed by damp has been most carefully restored by the tradesmen, who took casts from the south side and reproduced the decayed part on the north side in a manner which would take very sharp eyes to detect any difference between the two.[17]

The ceiling in the great hall which was described as hanging down in an alarming way was repaired by Currie with great resourcefulness. Robert Lorimer made a note of his method at the end of the 'Red Book'. Currie 'fixed railway rods across the room above and drew up the ceiling to this; he then placed a new floor on the bedroom above, with space between it and the old floor so that no weight should touch it. His ingenious device has held good during all the 38 years of the lease.'[18]

When Professor Lorimer died in 1890, the value of the work he instigated at Kellie was fully appreciated in terms of the then current Arts and Crafts principles:

> The painted panelling, plaster ceilings, woodwork, balustrades, doors, moulded architraves, iron work, hinges, locks, bolts and triling pins were all recognized and appreciated and what was wanting supplied in the style of the rest and so far as possible out of genuinely antique materials.[19]

The report points to the significance of the restoration of Kellie Castle by Professor Lorimer as a pioneer in terms of the restorations undertaken at the end of the nineteenth century by the Arts and Crafts architects. Such a restoration of a domestic building carried out at this date represented an extraordinary achievement. Perhaps financial constraints prevented a more thorough refurbishing of the castle, or perhaps, as it was to be primarily a summer residence for the Lorimers to complement their modern Baronial revival house in Edinburgh, they were willing to sacrifice a little comfort in a dwelling which would not be occupied all year round, little comforts which included a mains water supply and gas lighting.

It is equally conceivable that Professor Lorimer, well read and of diverse interests, was aware of and sympathetic to the ideas of Ruskin, Morris and the SPAB. He certainly held strong views on the task of restoring the castle. Ruskin was acquainted with Professor Blackie in Edinburgh, who was a close friend of Lorimer's by the 1870s. In his younger days, James Lorimer was involved with the Architectural Institute of Scotland. In 1850, he acted as convener of the committee for establishing a chair of architecture, and in 1853 a paper by him was read on *The Ecclesiastical Architecture of the Rhenish Provinces*.[20] Whatever the true reasons were for such a remarkable restoration, it proved crucial to the development of Robert Lorimer's career.

Robert Lorimer's own important contribution to castle restoration was first exemplified at Earlshall, Fife, in 1891 and subsequently at Dunderave, Argyll, in 1911 and Balmanno, Perthshire, in 1916. His achievements in sensitive restoring have led many to emphasise the importance of his early contact with Kellie. While this cannot be underestimated, it must be remembered that Robert Lorimer was only fourteen years old when the Kellie restoration began, and that when the commission for Earlshall was secured his early experiences had been supplemented by a distinctly varied apprenticeship. During this time, he was brought into contact with Hew Wardrop, Robert Rowand Anderson and, in London, with Bodley and the work of James MacLaren.

Lorimer always acknowledged his respect for Hew Wardrop, and in many ways his practice in later years can be seen as a continuation of the tradition of James Maitland Wardrop, Hew's father. In 1869, Wardrop and Brown had carried out the restrained restoration of Castle Stewart, Inverness-shire, where the only visible alterations to the exterior were the additions of an open-work tower, battlemented parapet and bartizans on the south-west tower. Most importantly, the interior plan was not altered. Here, as at Kellie, the castle was not continuously occupied but nevertheless maintained in reasonable repair.

With Rowand Anderson, Lorimer would have gained experience on the restoration of Dunblane Cathedral, which was in progress from 1889 to 1893. The governing principle of the restoration was sound historical research. As Lorimer recalled of Anderson:

> 'Go and analyse the old Scotch buildings' he used to say, 'study them as a medical student has to study anatomy, study the plan, see how the exterior is the natural expression of the interior, see how the later type of plan is a development of the earlier, look at the character of the masonry, measure the mouldings and plot them full size, and if you study the old buildings in this fashion it is conceivable you may one day become an architect, but remember, if you sit down in front of these old buildings and content yourself with making pretty water colour sketches of them, you never will.'[21]

Lorimer interpreted Morris's philosophy of design in his own terms:

> The whole gospel of modern design is to express the innate beauty of the materials used . . . go at design from the point of view of the material—make marble look like marble, oak like oak, glass like glass, copper like copper.[22]

In the context of restoration, Lorimer's comments on Morris as one of the prime movers in the SPAB are particularly interesting:

> This society was formed to try and stay the hand of the so-called restorer. I hope you all agree with me that it is quite impossible to restore an old Gothic building. You can mend it, you can keep it in repair and prevent it from falling down, but to restore it is and always will be absolutely impossible. The life and traditions that gave it being are gone, and can never return—you might as well try to re-galvanize a dead horse.[23]

This was precisely the approach which Lorimer took to his first great restoration project at Earlshall. Here, Lorimer was acknowldged for the delicacy of his approach and for refraining from superimposing new work on old. He also retained the weathered rubble masonry instead of replacing the harling which at one time covered the walls.

Earlshall castle was acquired by R.W. Mackenzie, a family friend of the Lorimers, and Robert Lorimer was offered the job of restoring it while he was still in London in 1891. The condition of the building was similar to that in which Kellie had been when the Lorimers first found it, and the scheme of restoration carried out at Earlshall closely echoes Professor Lorimer's restoration of Kellie. The emphasis was on repair rather than replacement. Robert Lorimer's largest contributions to the main building were on the scale of small Arts and Crafts-style coloured glass windows lighting the turnpike stair, and the carved wooden screen in the great hall, which he modelled on the screen at Falkland Palace.

Lorimer's drawing for the wood panelling and plaster ceiling in one of the tower rooms shows the influence of the vine room at Kellie. The ancillary buildings which he added set the pattern for future garden buildings. The bell-roofed summerhouse recurs in many later commissions.

As Peter Savage has noted, Lorimer claimed that only work which remained 'clearly legible' was retouched and that no attempt was made to fill in parts which had disappeared, which would have destroyed the character of the old.[24] The painted ceiling in the gallery had suffered severely in some places, but more than enough of it survived to make extensive new work unnecessary. The tenor of the restoration can be more readily appreciated by comparison with an earlier, unexecuted scheme by W.F. Lyon, which comprised drastic rebuilding and extensions.

In the spring of 1893, Lorimer conducted a tour around Earlshall for members of the Edinburgh Architectural Association, ensuring that his early work gained equally early appreciation from his professional colleagues.

After Professor Lorimer's death in 1890, John Henry took over as leesee of Kellie Castle, and in 1897 Robert Lorimer undertook further restoration work there on a larger scale. He first directed his attention to the drawing room and described the work in a letter to his friend Dods:

> I must tell you about the drawing room at Kellie. We got sick of that yellow paper pasted over the panelling etc., so resolved to have it off. Had a man along who tore off the whole thing and disclosed panelling, most of it of the consistency of buttery oat cakes . . . well, during the spring time we had the Wheelers turned on and started mending away and panelled some bits where there was just canvas before and faked up various bits and got the Clows to carve a smacking cartouche with our crest to stick against the cornice of the chimney piece, the centre one with the Misters initials and the two side ones with Batistes and mine. Then you'll remember that over the side chimney piece there was a whacking panel where a picture had been the old days afore-time, well, we've put bolection moulding round this, and stretched a canvas on it and John Henry has asked Mrs Traquair to paint a picture on it, which she's agreed to do particularly. Won't that be ripping having that dear little lady staying in this house for about a month, painting this. We've mended the panelling everywhere except on the north wall where you'll remember there had evidently been a huge tapestry panel.[25]

This letter is illuminating in its suggestion of the differences in taste between Professor

Lorimer and his son. In the 'Red Book', Professor Lorimer expressed his dislike of the panelling in the drawing room, preferring the richer, earlier forms of Scottish decoration, in line with the prevalent high Victorian Gothic taste. In contrast, Robert Lorimer allied himself with the Arts and Crafts taste, echoing Morris's call for simplicity in interior decoration, with plain white walls interrupted only by what was functional or beautiful. He added four cartouches carved by the Clows, three of which are situated above the fireplace on the south wall and one above the fireplace on the east wall. The Clows also used a small carved panel with a cherry motif to enliven the north wall. It was presumably at this time that Lorimer altered the fireplace on the south wall, adding the antique Dutch tiles, of which he was fond, which he introduced to many of his domestic commissions.

Leslie Thomson, in his article on Robert Lorimer written shortly after the latter's death, noted that:

> Sir Robert Lormier's basic idea in dealing with such a case as Dunderave
> was to let the old building stand out and tell its own story. Making the
> additions, while being carried out with similar materials and detail to the
> old work and so generally harmonizing with it, stand confessed as the
> work of a different age.[26]

Dunderave presented a greater challenge than Earlshall in that it was just a shell when Lorimer was commissioned to restore it in 1911. The ruined castle was owned by the Nobles; Sir Andrew Noble had commissioned Lorimer to build a new mansion house on his estate in 1906, which resulted in the massive house of Ardkinglas. Dunderave is a breathtaking place. Lorimer maximised the dramatic site wedged onto the shore of Loch Fyne and, with clever trickery, maintained the uncompromising wall faces while adapting the building to modern requirements. The wings, both L-plan, were kept low, not to detract from the stark effect of height in the old tower and to keep them in scale with the entrance. The entrance was something of the star attraction at Dunderave. The main door was framed with lavish carving, and over the door the date of 1596 was inscribed.

It was also at Dunderave that, as Thomson noted, we have 'an example of the extraordinary care and thoroughness which Lorimer lavished on his work where full sized canvas models were made of the additions which were shifted about till a suitable disposition was arrived at'. The technique would seem to have paid off, and it is easy to imagine Lorimer revelling in creating a composition which appeared to erupt out of the earth and the water in this grim local stone.

In the interiors of Dunderave, Lorimer was able to indulge his delight in craftsmanship, from the rough-hewn oak beams of the dining-room ceiling to the plasterwork, notably in the barrel-vaulted sitting room, which revived the patterns and methods of the seventeenth-century Scottish ceilings epitomised at Kellie.

Had it not been for the Great War, the chances are that Kellie Castle would have supplied much greater evidence of Robert Lorimer's architectural intervention. Walter Henry Erskine, who had originally negotiated Kellie's lease with Professor Lorimer, died in 1888 and his heir, Walter John Francis Erskine, was apparently more anxious to profit from his inherited property. In 1915, a year before the lease was due to expire, the new Earl of Mar and Kellie contacted Robert Lorimar to say that he intended to carry out a full renovation of Kellie and asked Robert to act as his architect.

It is not surprising to find that Lorimer responded to the suggestion with alacrity. The plan he drew up and the description he gave in correspondence with the Earl illustrate a scheme of modernisation and alteration which are sympathetic while giving the whole a definite Lorimer stamp. Based very closely on the work he had done at Dunderave, the plans hinged on the extension of the stable offices added by his father. By adding rooms to the attic storey and raising the height of the buildings by some five feet, the alterations would have provided a series of rooms around the existing courtyard. A corridor to the north would have linked the wing with the main building and, by extending westwards, the whole courtyard could be enclosed, leaving an archway with rusticated voussoirs in the centre. There was to be another crow-stepped gable on the east elevation and dormer windows piercing the roofline throughout. However, with the continuing war and the escalation of prices which followed in 1918, these plans were finally abandoned.

In 1916, the Glasgow ship merchant W.A. Miller commissioned Lorimer to remodel Balmanno Castle in Perthshire. Balmanno makes a suitable climax to Lorimer's career in castle restorations; of all the jobs he had ever done, Balmanno was reputed to be the one he would have liked to live in. The choice of harling here lent unity to a building successively added to during the seventeenth and eighteenth centuries and imposed a Lorimerian sixteenth-century character to the whole. New service quarters were added in a low, two-storey wing. An entrance lodge was placed across the approach which had a central archway, producing a picturesque dark frame for the east facade of the castle.

As at Dunderave, the commission was a generous one. Lorimer was requested not only to restore the castle but also to furnish the interior and lay out the gardens. The interior scheme included designs for many items of furniture as well as wood panelling and enriched plaster ceilings. A variety of indigenous woods were used to good effect at a time when such materials were in short supply.

Lorimer is already well known to many. In his lifetime, he was undoubtedly more financially successful than Mackintosh, but that was hardly difficult. They both had their roots in Scottish domestic architecture of the sixteenth century and the example of James MacLaren fixed in their minds, but, while Mackintosh took the vernacular path to modernism, Lorimer found his strength in an Arts and Crafts ability to exhort fine work from fine craftsmen and imbue it with a Scottish spirit.

This chapter is based on a paper delivered by Harriet Richardson at the conference 'Mackintosh and his Successful Contemporaries'.

Royal Commission for Ancient and Historic Monuments

NOTES

1. P. Savage, *Lorimer and the Edinburgh Craft Designers*, Edinburgh, 1980.

2. B. Ferry, *Recollections of A.C. Pugin and A.W.N. Pugin*, London, 1861, p. 156.

3. G.G. Scott, 'On the Conservation of Ancient Architectural Monuments and Remains', *Transactions of the RIBA*, 1st Series, XXII, 1862.

4. F. Grose, *Antiquities of Scotland*, 2 volumes, London, 1789–91.

5. R.W. Billings, *The Baronial and Ecclesiastical Antiquities of Scotland*, vol. I, Edinburgh, 1848, introduction.

6. Ibid.

7. J. Ruskin, 'The Lamp of Memory', *Seven Lamps of Architecture*, London, 1990, p. 339.

8. J. Ruskin, attrib. Memorandum, 1 May 1855, Society of Antiquities, quoted in J. Fawcett (ed.), *The Future of the Past*, London, 1976, p. 50.

9. J. Ruskin, 'The Lamp of Memory', *Seven Lamps of Architecture*, London, 1900, p. 355.

10. W. Morris, speech at Annual Meeting of SPAB, 1877.

11. R.W. Billings, *The Baronial and Ecclesiastical Antiquities of Scotland*, vol. I, Edinburgh, 1848, introduction.

12. D. Macgibbon and T. Ross, *Castellated and Domestic Architecture of Scotland*, vol. II, Edinburgh, 1887, pp. 125–33.

13. J. Lorimer, *Red Book of Kellie*, n.d., unpublished manuscript.

14. A. Diston, *Antiquities of Fife*, Cupar, 1866.

15. J.A. Lorimer, *The Family History*, n.d., unpublished manuscript.

16. SRO Erskine family papers. Letter from James Lorimer to W.R. Kermack, solicitor, 1 June 1878. GD.124/17.

17. *The East of Fife Record*, 24 October 1879.

18. J. Lorimer, *Red Book of Kellie*, addition in pencil by Robert Lorimer.

19. *The East of Fife Record*, 21 February 1890.

20. J. Lorimer, 'The Ecclesiastical Architecture of the Rhenish Provinces', *Proceedings of the Architectural Institute of Scotland*, 1853.

21. R. Lorimer, 'The Works and Influence of William Morris', paper delivered to Edinburgh Architectural Association, 1897, unpublished manuscript.

22. Ibid.

23. Ibid.

24. P. Savage, *Robert Lorimer and the Edinburgh Craft Designers*, Edinburgh, 1980, p. 9.

25. P. Savage, *Robert Lorimer and the Edinburgh Craft Designers*, Ph.D. thesis, Edinburgh University, 1973.

26. L.G. Thomson, 'Robert Lorimer', *QIAS*, Autumn 1929.

Millionayrshire Mansions

The county of Ayrshire provided a lucrative source of commissions for the architects of Mackintosh's day, drawing on local firms and on significant names from Edinburgh and Glasgow. This chapter provides a brief introduction to the building of country houses in the area between 1890 and 1914. Since Ayrshire represents a large and varied slice of Scottish topography and social life, the country houses erected in that period are not only interesting for their own sakes, but also can be used as a case study of relevance to the understanding of Scottish late Victorian and Edwardian taste in country-house architecture as a whole.[1]

AYRSHIRE'S position on the Glasgow riviera, with golf providing an additional attraction to the pleasures of country life, made it ideal for the rich industrialists of the west of Scotland, many of whom went as far 'doon the watter' as possible in an almost symbolic effort at gentrification. It was these men, along with the richest of the more established families, who put the million into Millionayrshire.

Such an influx of wealth was not wholly new to Ayrshire: the pattern of country estates being bought in the county with new money earned elsewhere goes back to the eighteenth century.[2] What was certainly new was the nature of response from architects. This can be illustrated by comparing a house like Doonside (Figure 6.1), near Alloway, designed by J. MacVicar Anderson, with Chapeltoun House, near Stewarton (Figure 6.2) designed by Alexander Cullen. Anderson's design clearly betrays his background in William Burn's office. It is derived from the classic 'corridor plan' and is in a crisp English Jacobean style typical of the Burn and Bryce school which dominated Scottish architecture until the 1870s. Chapeltoun was built for Hugh Neilson, owner of the Summerlee Iron Company, in an up-to-date 'Arts and Crafts'-influenced idiom. Its low-slung massing and use of harled brick with stone detailing contrasts with the more formal essay in ashlar of the earlier house and evokes a vision of a past characterised more by the sturdy yeoman than the haughty aristocrat.

Even while Doonside was being built, however, Arts and Crafts ideas were beginning to make themselves felt in Ayrshire. James A. Morris, an Ayr architect who seems to have spent a lot of his time in London, built a number of suburban mansions in Ayr during the 1880s and 1890s.[3] The real explosion of Arts and Crafts-inspired work, however, occurred after 1898. In that year, William Leiper produced a charming (sub-Shaw) half-timbered manor at Piersland on the fringes of Troon for the whisky baron, Sir

6.1. J. MacVicar Anderson, Doonside House, 1884–9, demolished 1961. A typical Jacobean style country house from the Burn and Bryce School. (RCAHMS)

Alexander Walker. In both its style and location, Piersland was a significant premonition of Edwardian taste. Deliberately exploiting the intimate, vernacular and picturesque charm of 'Old English' without any real attempt to mislead the unsuspecting, Piersland was a country house only in its style and associations; in reality it was an ornate golfing box conveniently placed for access to the course.

There were many to whom the mystique and prestige of country life appealed but who were not yet prepared to lose themselves in it; hence the astonishing development of South Wood at Troon, a complete suburb composed exclusively of large and imposing mansions set in policies which, though not ungenerous, often relied on belts of planting to block out the view of the neighbouring pile. Likewise, the railway at Skelmorlie gave

6.2. Alexander Cullen, Chapeltoun House, 1908–10. Showing some influence of Arts and Crafts ideas. (Author)

birth to Upper Skelmorlie, providing gentrified residences and sea breezes (but no golf) for wealthy commuters who wished to be within easy reach of their offices and boardrooms in Glasgow and who had no desire to be encumbered with the responsibilities or expense of a country estate.

Although styles based on English vernacular architecture were popular with many architects, James Miller was a particularly enthusiastic advocate. At Monktonhead (1910), near Troon, he ran the full gamut of materials and textures available to such work from half-timbering and tall brick chimneys, through bricks laid in herringbone pattern, down to hanging tiles, roof tiles and a visual equivalent of exterior plaster. The grandest of his houses, evocative of England's manorial past, was Kildonan (1910–23), near Barrhill. Begun on the eve of the Great War for Captain Euan Wallace (an MP who inherited a large portion of south Ayrshire and evidently did not wish that his stay there should be at all purgatorial), this is a distinctly revivalist creation, 'perhaps the last great country house in the gothic revival tradition'[4] decked out in Cotswold Tudor style. But Kildonan, though thoroughly revivalist, was also modern in that there was no self-conscious attempt at instant age, a point worth making in respect of all the new houses considered in this survey. In comparison with many other Ayrshire clients, Captain Wallace moved in a higher stratum of society. His house, therefore, had to be a reflection of his prestige and, possibly, his political ambition. Consequently, it was built for show, for entertainment, for huge house parties, for an army of servants and not as a home. It was an expression of power made venerable and sociable by the use of English manorial forms.

Rather more forward-looking in style than Kildonan is Blanefield, near Kirkoswald, a more modest but equally streamlined white mansion of 1913 designed by Miller in a very suave modern Tudor style. The entrance feature at Blanefield, in cream-coloured stone, is manorial (if unexceptional when compared with Kildonan); but the garden front is exceedingly sleek, in bands of dark roofing slate, white rendered first floor, and cream stonework on the ground floor. Even more free and 'contemporary' in their handling are the attractive, clean and functional lines of the detached ancillary buildings at Blanefield and the superb stable block at Kildonan.

It is, however, Turnberry Hotel, completed in 1906, which perhaps best demonstrates Miller's inspired ability to handle an enormous composition (the rationale for which was significantly provided by a combination of railway transport and golf), integrating the apparatus of English revival styles in a dazzling and free manner rather beyond the reach of mere historicism alone.

Revivalism of one form or another was generally adhered to in Ayrshire mansions. At South Wood, Sandhill, possibly the earliest of all the South Wood mansions, is red brick with red roof tiles, and possibly French in inspiration. Southpark (1910), also brick with inset patterns in flint, is of a more positively English character. Auchenkyle (c. 1900) is pure Queen Anne in red brick again, while Grey Gables (Figure 6.3) is modern Tudor or Elizabethan, its white bargeboards seeming to link hands over its garden front.

The architect of none of these houses is known, though Grey Gables may be the work of James Miller or even of H.E. Clifford. Clifford's often inspired and sometimes quirky hand is easier to spot in the bizarre gables and porch of Craigend, near Troon (demolished c. 1986), and probably at Cragston (c. 1900), a mill-owner's house near Stewarton which boasts similarly freakish gables. At Monkton Hall (c. 1912) in South Wood, Clifford produced real Hansel and Gretel stuff, with outlandish details derived somewhat tortuously from Old English work. Only the all-encompassing grey harl softens in any way the startling disjunction between forms on the garden front, where triangular gablets sit on rounded bows while a verandah, with the crudest of balustrading, is supported uneasily on four contrastingly elegant columns.

Outside Troon's well-heeled suburbs, Ayr architect James Kennedy Hunter, former partner of James A. Morris, was producing country houses which were very up-to-date, using harl as an almost total exterior wall-covering, offering clients an effect as 'artistic' as it was cost-effective. Black Clauchrie (Figure 6.4), dating from the turn of the century, is probably the earliest of these houses and is a very stylish shooting lodge on a high, lonely moor above Barrhill. Next was Templetonburn (1901 and 1908) at the

6.3. Architect unknown, Grey Gables, 1908–9. Typical of many Ayrshire houses of this time in its use of an English style. (Author)

heart of an estate near Kilmarnock; then High Greenan (1910) on the edge of a coastal heath near Ayr; and finally The Croft (1912) on the outskirts of Dalry. With these houses, and in many of his smaller villas, Hunter worked in a consistent style (perhaps sub-Voysey in very general character), though sometimes, as at Black Clauchrie and Templetonburn, introducing Scottish details such as crow steps. If at the kennels and ancillary buildings at Black Clauchrie the end result looked depressingly like a premonition of a 1920s economy-minded state school, greater concentration on detailing and harmonious design at the main house make it—inside and out—probably Hunter's most successful creation; and one glimpses something of the artistic achievement of the age when one realises that a relatively unknown provincial architect and a compliantly wealthy client could come up with this.

Hunter's High Greenan earns its laurels in an equally Arts and Crafts interplay of gables and sloping roofs which are delicately swept as they reach the wallhead—a game which Hunter also played at The Croft—but the interior of High Greenan is less lavish and of lesser quality than Black Clauchrie; presumably an indication of less generous interest on the part of the client.

Whatever quality as good, well-designed and pleasing architecture the houses we have already examined possess, it is painfully obvious that, while the architects of the South had succeeded in developing their vernacular tradition into a modern style, these Scottish architects were merely catering to their clients by importing the fashionable

6.4. James A. Hunter, Black Clauchrie, c. 1900: entrance, front; garden, front; drawing room; dining room (Mr & Mrs Watts of Black Clauchrie).

styles of England. Although there had been a clearly discernible movement away from the strict 'trammels of style', partly influenced by the Arts and Crafts movement and partly by a desire to introduce Scottish features for variation, such a superficial tinkering could not alter the fact that the examples we have looked at are steadfastly English first and Scottish later.

There were of course problems in designing in a more purely Scottish style at the turn of the century, since the original style of towers, fortified houses and even 'palace' ranges was perhaps least suited to translation to the requirements of large and necessarily sprawling country houses. Consequently, additions made to Newark Castle (James Miller, 1907–8) and to Blair Castle (Leadbetter and Fairlie, 1893) adopted a watered-down High Victorian Scottish Baronial, unturreted and somewhat tame. The 'charm of unpretentious old Scottish buildings, with their honest plainness and simple, almost rugged massiveness'[5] was rather better captured, however, in smaller mansions such as Balnowlart (Figure 6.5) by J. Jerdan and Sons, where the entrance drive approaches the gable end of the house, the small windows and massive chimney of which unmistakeably suggest a Scottish fortified house. Deasholm (T. Andrew Millar, 1912) is a little larger and slightly over-contrived in its picturesque corner tower, but successfully blends Scottish 'vernacular' of various periods in a particularly stylish way. John A. Campbell's

6.5. J. Jerdan & Sons, Balnowlart 1905. One of a number of Ayrshire houses of this period
inspired by Scottish castellated architecture. (Author)

masterly Southwood House, despite its rather manorial sprawl, displays Scottish style
carved detail set against the harl of its walls: its style may be a rather rarified late 'Old
Scots' of seventeenth-century origin, hence the juxtaposition of piended and crowstep-
gabled roofs.

At Rowallan (designed 1901–2) near Kilmaurs, Robert Lorimer succeeded in creating
a Scottish Baronial pile in which the brutality of the High Victorian Baronial manner was
drowned in a flood of mellifluous ogee curves and in which considerable effort was taken
to capture the spirit of the old work in a manner clearly inspired by Auchans rather than
by Old Rowallan nearby. In similar taste, perhaps, is J.K. Hunter's polished reconstruction of the parapet and garret of St John's Tower (1914) in Ayr: congruous and
appropriate, though surely not intended to deceive.

The desire to convince, if not actually to deceive, is certainly present in Ayrshire's
examples of the restorations of old Scottish buildings carried out during this period. To
some extent conjectural or even imaginative, the massive and beautifully-crafted restoration of Dean Castle (1908–46) near Kilmarnock, and the more diminutively-scaled
restoration (c. 1895) and delightful extension (James Chalmers, 1910) of Kirkland in

Dunlop were uncomprising in their pursuit of a dream-like vision of the past and were more convincing in their vernacular handling than the completely new Scottish-style houses.

Lucrative in commissions, often from the up-and-coming (or incoming) rich; distinctly different in their handling of revivalist styles from that which had gone before; and distinguished by exceptional attention to quality of design and detail, but obsessively devoted to (largely English-manorial-inspired) evocations of styles of the past, the mansions of Ayrshire in the years between 1890 and 1914 were a triumph of delight, emblematic of a halcyon Indian summer of too much good taste and, for some, too much easy money. But is any deeper explanation possible, and what real architectural or artistic significance should one attach to this phenomenon?

Part of the answer is to be found at Noddsdale, a country house near Largs remodelled in Old English style during the Twenties by Fryers and Penman for John M. Robertson, a fastidious client who ordered a large number of measured drawings for consideration, some showing only the slightest variation of internal detailing. Robertson's library still contains volumes with slips of paper (one of them being a piece of Fryers and Penman headed notepaper) inserted at pages showing illustrations of Old English work which he particularly admired. Such an exacting enthusiasm dramatically highlights the infatuation of clients and the easy familiarity of architects with the styles revealed through such publications as *Country Life* or *The Studio* which, themselves the product as much as the instrument of the popularised Arts and Crafts movement, communicated to Scotland the stylish work of the South, where it was taken up often before or even in preference to the exploitation of Scotland's own architectural vernacular.

Seen in terms of the 'progress' of Scottish architecture, and compared with the achievement of Mackintosh, such work as that in Ayrshire may seem to occupy only a cul-de-sac in architectural history; but its worth in a less 'evolutionary' perspective was profound. To such a contemporary as Hermann Muthesius, who acknowledged Mackintosh as a key figure of his age, the domestic work of Mackintosh's more commercially successful contemporaries was of serious importance, and their achievement worthy of emulation.[6] In the years before the Great War, country-house commissions were not yet widely seen as either a social or an artistic irrelevance, and for architects it was often considered work of high prestige (it being such work which they tended to exhibit).

Finally, perhaps a revealing clue as to how country-house architecture fitted into the wider context of contemporary mainstream artistic sensibility can be provided by a browse through the annual volumes of *Academy Architecture* for this period. After the pages in which Scottish architects exhibited mouth-wateringly attractive drawings for their work, there often follows a section devoted exclusively to the work of sculptors. Here, to one's astonishment, is found illustrated a high proportion of sleek, nubile and, it must be said erotic statuary. Nymphs disport themselves, scorning fig leaves; mythological maidens are chained to rocks; and figures symbolic of certain virtues or properties seem to testify only to the alarmingly defective capacities of the Edwardian bodice. But no matter how direct the appeal to the senses of such work, there is a delicacy, a grace and an overriding quality of design and execution which prevents a descent—even when imbued with what may seem today to be a slightly dubious taste—into the pornographic, the vulgar or the base. Perhaps it is in terms of a comparably direct appeal that we should understand the highly appealing but never cloying revivalism and Arts and Crafts-inflenced country-house work which we have examined. Like the statuary, such houses are just as consummately crafted in design, materials and execution, and in their own way are every bit as 'sexy'.

This chapter is based on a paper delivered by Mike Davis at the conference 'Mackintosh and his Successful Contemporaries'.

Reid Kerr College, Paisley

ACKNOWLEDGEMENTS

I am indebted to Rob Close, who very kindly contributed the fruits of his own extensive research on the dating and attribution of the buildings of this period.

NOTES

1. More detailed treatment of this subject can be found in Michael C. Davis *The Castles and Mansions of Ayrshire*, Michael C. Davis, 1990.

2. Eighteenth-century examples of new money being invested in Ayrshire estates are the Oswalds of Auchencruive and the Alexanders of Balloch-myle, whose fortunes were based on foreign trade and industry.

3. Rob Close 'Attainable Ideals: James A. Morris, 1857–1942', in *Charles Rennie Mackintosh Society Newsletter* 28, November 1986.

4. Clive Aslet *The Last Country Houses*, Newhaven, Yale University Press, 1982, p. 321.

5. Hermann Muthesius *The English House*, (Berlin, 1904, 2nd edition Leipzig 1908–11), p. 62.

6. Ibid.

William Kerr

A self-effacing architect of real quality, William Kerr trained under J.J.
Burnet in Glasgow, was assistant to T.G. Abercrombie in Paisley, and then
for four decades was senior partner in the firm of John Melvin and Son,
Alloa. His repertoire included major commercial buildings, country houses,
public buildings, villas . . . , mastered in the style of the day: Edwardian
Baroque, Arts and Crafts, or Thirties 'Moderne'.

WILLIAM KERR was born in Houston, Renfrewshire, on 23 June
1866. His fatter was a master joiner, working from his yard behind the family home,
Cotswold, in South Street. Cotswold is part of a long row still known as Kerr's Land,
and it was here that William Kerr lived until sometime after his marriage in the late
1890s.

In 1885, he began a five-year apprenticeship in Glasgow with John James Burnet. He
probably worked in Glasgow on Burnet and Campbell's Barony Church (1886–9),
perhaps the most important Victorian Gothic Church in Scotland, the Beaux-Arts-
inspired Athenaeum (1886), and from 1887 to 1889, on the drawings of what was the
first of Burnet's series of squat-towered 'Arts and Crafts Gothic' churches, St Molio's
Church at Shiskine, on Arran.

In 1890, Kerr went to work as principal assistant to Thomas Graham Abercrombie of
Paisley, remaining there until 1902. A number of buildings designed by the Abercrombie
office at that time owe much to Kerr. Most were in Paisley, and designed in a very
Scottish classical style, with Arts and Crafts overtones. There were many prestigious
commissions, but also a large number of tenements, small houses, additions, etc., as with
any local practice.

The original Royal Alexandra Infirmary was designed by the Abercrombie office over
a period of six years (1894–1900). The main block has an E-shape plan with massive,
overscaled, semicircular, Doric-columned verandahs to each wing, rather plain elevations, and interest added to the roofline by pedimented half-dormers, cupola ventilators,
square water tower, and turrets. The Nurses' Home (1898 and extensions) is very Scots,
with drum turrets flanking the entrance (perhaps derivative of Falkland), with a balcony
above. The Dispensary and Lodge (1898–9) fronts the main road, with tall pedimented
windows, gables and arches.

The tall, symmetrically-fronted Territorial Army Drill Hall (1896) is set in a prime
location next to the Coats Memorial Baptist Church, and has stylistic similarities to the

Royal Alexandra Infirmary, through with a plain, twin-gabled palace front, pedimented dormers, cupola and Drumlanrig-like corner turrets.

Whiteleigh (c. 1896) is a red and white asymmetrical villa which has many similarities with the much later English suburban-style villas designed by Kerr in Alloa. It has half-timbered decoration, a large, bow-windowed corner tower and an Italianate low pyramid-roofed belvedere. More Scots is the Peter Brough Nurses' Home, Oakshaw Street (1897), now student residences, dominated by a tall, three-storey entrance tower, and with pedimented dormers, though the gatepiers date from an earlier house.

One of the last major Paisley projects that Kerr would likely have worked on was Crosbie (1901–2), a delightful, vast, L-plan mansion, in scale with its time. The elevations are more regular, but elements such as the Ionic-style main entrance porch in the re-entrant can be followed through from The Sanctuary to later projects such as The Gean and the Walker Institute extension (see below). Typically eclectic, Crosbie has plain, huge chimney stacks; low, leaded windows under overhanging eves; diagonally opposite, corbelled, battlemented turrets; steep, skewed gables; and mullioned and transomed bays. Finished in a traditional Scots grey harl, with cream sandstone details, this house compares well with any by the majority of better-known contemporary architects.

Thread was the principal product of Paisley's vast cotton-spinning industry, dominated by the Coats and Clark families. Further east, one of the principal industries of the much smaller town of Alloa was John Paton and Sons' woollen yarn factories, by this time run by the Forrester-Paton family. The Coats and Forrester-Paton families were no doubt known to each other long before the massive Coats-Paton merger, and it is known that Abercrombie was friendly with the Coats family, spending holidays with them, especially on their yacht.

At the turn of the century, Alexander Forrester-Paton wanted a talented architect to design his Kilncraigs factory offices, but did not consider any of the existing local firms suitable. Thus in 1902 he brought Kerr to Alloa to join John Melvin junior (1855–1905) as a partner in the long-established practice of John Melvin and Son, and awarded that firm the commission.

The Forrester-Patons were keen supporters of the Liberal Party, the YMCA, the United Presbyterian Church, local School Boards and the local Temperance Movement. It must have been encouraging to them that Kerr was also abstinent (indeed, at his eldest son's wedding, no-one was brave enough to tell him that what he thought was particularly good lemonade was actually champagne).

When Kerr arrived in Alloa, Melvin was working on a series of large houses on Claremont. The Parish Church Manse, now Claremont House (1901–2), has a simple south front, with twin canted bay windows, built without their high roofs shown on surviving early (Melvin?) drawings. The north, or entrance, front is more disjointed,

7.1. William Kerr, Kilncraigs offices, 1902–4. The Edwardian baroque offices which Kerr was brought to Alloa to design by Alexander Forrester-Paton. (Clackmannan District Council)

with gable, porch, north wing and west wing. The porch doubles as a balcony to the first floor, and above its door is a panel flanked by two sea serpents.

Next door is Craig-na-Aird (1902), with a similar south front, but less interesting north or entrance fronts. Next to that, Craigmyle (1902) also has a similar plan and south front. This time the entrance front incorporates a three-storey round tower in its re-entrant, and has a simple, timber-columned, open porch. It is equally disjointed, but somehow a more pleasing composition.

Meanwhile, Kerr was designing a far more important work, his *raison d'être* in Alloa being to provide Paton's yarn mills with prestigious new offices. The Kilncraigs Offices (1902–4: Figure 7.1) is a thirteen-by-five-bay, flamboyant Baroque palace, ornamented with tall arched windows, Ionic pilasters and, for the final built design, broken scrolled pediments. Internal enrichments include fine wainscoting and a marble staircase.

His next building was also commissioned by Alexander Forrester-Paton, the Alloa Liberal Club (1903–4), using a superb combination of Jacobean and Arts and Crafts styles. In the roof is a vaulted billiards room with sculpted dormer windows and balconies; the first floor is the main hall, its tall mullioned bay windows featuring stained-glass scenes of Alloa by Oscar Paterson of Glasgow. The ground floor was intended as club offices, but was soon equipped as an architects' office and used by successive partners in John Melvin and Son, until the last partner's retiral in 1985.

The whole building contains subtly crafted fittings. Kerr's own office retains its glazed-screen partitions and fitted secretary's (or partner's?) office. The building was latterly acquired by the District Council, first providing an exhibition gallery and library accommodation, and more recently and fittingly in use as the District Architects' office. The drawing office lost its purpose-designed fitments to storage for possible reuse in Bo'ness.

In 1905, Melvin died, and so Kerr became the sole partner. The villas on Claremont continued with a manse for the Moncrieff United Free Church (another Forrester-Paton connection), next to Craigmyle on Claremont. This is now Struan House (1904–5), a residential school for autistic children. Struan is more typically Scots and free of stylistic restraints than the previous Claremont villas, which perhaps had been caused by Melvin's influence. This is a white rendered L-plan house with prominent skewed gables, and exposed stone margins and date panels, referring to the grander houses of previous centuries, yet still eclectic with its contemporary English red tiled roof.

Also in 1905, Kerr designed Kellyside, for a bleachworks owner, on the outskirts of Dollar. Kellyside is very English, breaking with all local tradition in its use of red brick, now dulled with the patina of time, and still delights as a fine example of a small Arts and Crafts mansion. Bay windows rising to separate gables, oriel windows, small rectangular dormers, half-timbered gables, a recessed arched porch, the immaculate brickwork, and above all the huge, rambling slate roof, all combine to compose a building which reflects the work of architects like Lutyens, Voysey and Shaw.

Glenvar (1908) is a subdued, smaller version of Kellyside, set into the hillside near the entrance to Dollar Glen. It has a double-gabled frontage of grey harled brickwork, with bay windows and a verandah, and with the main entrance through an integral arched porch to the west. The design was again simplified in the same year to become the semidetached villa at 96–98 Tullibody Road, Alloa, built for the Forrester-Patons: a half-timber gabled precursor of Kerr's 1920s council housing.

A further example of a simple half-timber gable decorated cottage villa is 25 Alexandra Drive (1910), Alloa, which is enhanced by its gabled re-entrant stair tower and tall arched window. Meadowbank, Dollar (1934), very near Glenvar, was built for that houseowner's sister to a very similar design, nearly thirty years on. Meadowbank, though, has only one bay-windowed gable, and the entrance is back to the traditional centre of the frontage.

Lethangie House, Kinross, was a commission for the Tillicoultry branch of the Paton family. Originally acquired as a summer residence, it later replaced the Stirling and Tillicoultry houses as the main residence. To a modest vernacular farmhouse, on an older site which retains a good doocot, garden gazebo, heather summerhouse and Victorian

7.2. William Kerr, The Gean, Alloa, 1912–14, north elevation. Survey photography showing The Gean immediately prior to its recent conversion to a hotel and restraurant. (RCAHMS)

stableblock, Kerr added a 'U'-shaped rear wing, in 1911, which he had to rebuild and extend with a 'granny flat' following a fire in the 1930s. The house combines classical details, such as a porticoed hallway reminiscent of that at Kinross House, with well-proportioned rooms, Arts and Crafts detailing, and Kerr's typical multi-paned windows looking into sunny gardens. The projecting west chimney with ingleneuk seating, staircases and galleries, and rear flat entrance, are particular features.

The Gean (Figure 7.2) (1912–14), was commissioned by the parents of Alexander Forrester-Paton as his wedding present, and Kerr met the challenge to provide his patrons with perhaps his most spectacular building. The Gean is a vast, Jacobean Arts and Crafts mansion, strongly influenced by Lutyens and skilfully detailed, inside and out.

In 1910, Kerr was called on to provide a matching extension to the County Buildings, Alloa, which had been designed by Brown and Wardrop (1863–4) in an imposing Franco-Gothic style. The match is so perfect, it is rather disappointing. He was much more adventurous in his later, Jacobean-style, Police Office extension of 1938. He provided a building that relates to its parent, yet has an identity of its own.

Sauchie Public Hall (1911 and 1925) was a major work and combines features which became hallmarks of Kerr's more neo-vernacular buildings: white harled walls, large hipped-roofed multi-paned bay windows, bell-shaped roof ventilators, curved 'Dutch'

7.3. The Townhead Institute, Drysdale Street, Alloa, 1914. Taken in the 1970s prior to insensitive conversion to shops and flats in the 1980s. (Clackmannan District Council)

gabled entrances, buttressing, leaded lights and a recessed archway. It was the precursor of the smaller versions at Fishcross Miner's Welfare Hall (1931) and the extension to Coalsnaughton Village Hall (1925), institutions vital to the impoverished local mining communities.

The Townhead Institute (1914; Figure 7.3) was built for Miss Catherine Forrester-Paton as Temperance YMCA clubrooms on the site of the popular 'Prince of Wales' tavern. The new building later revived its popularity as the 'Townhead Lunch and Tearooms', and now survives as shops and flats. Designed in Kerr's favourite red hipped-roofed, white-harled, mannered version of the Arts and Crafts style, at the corner of two principal streets, its quality was in the simplicity of materials, scale and proportion.

In 1919, the Walker Institute, Tillicoultry, reopened with added facilities, which included a new Classical Renaissance-style rear porch with dentil mouldings: a simple yet attractive addition.

After the 1914–18 War, Kerr was involved in designing the first housing schemes for the local Burgh Councils. The blocks were simple in proportion, materials and design, fitting comfortably into the existing townscapes. Most survive to this day, two- and four-house blocks characterised by the double-gabled frontages of harled brickwork, traditional astragaled sash-and-case windows, and slate roofs, and were built during the 1920s and 1930s on numerous sites throughout Clackmannanshire.

In 1912, Kerr had been joined by a new partner, his former apprentice John Gray (1878–1946), who then returned to the practice after serving in the Royal Engineers during the war. Gray was an experienced architect not without originality and talent himself, and he remained with the firm until his death. Almost all projects were attributed to the firm, rather than to individual architects, hence Gray was probably involved in many of the projects discussed in this chapter.

Although Kerr was responsible for the original design of several schools, Gray held the appointment of local Education Architect. There are many other buildings of a very similar style—Alloa Parish Church Hall (1926), the Alloa YMCA Hall, Mar Street (1936), Tillicoultry Primary School (1938), extensions to the Grange and Burgh Schools, Alloa, and the High School, Stirling. They relate to the series of Miners' Welfare buildings, begun with Kerr's Sauchie Hall, with their use of harled brickwork, large multi-paned windows, hugh bay windows, wide overhanging eaves and feature roof ventilators.

The Patons commissioned yet another building, Paton's and Baldwin's Sports Pavilion (1926), on land near The Gean. The Pavilion consists of a white, harled, wide, 'H'-shaped block, with lighthouse-like, bell-roofed, octagonal stair towers marking the corners. Between the wings is a low, glazed verandah with a strip of multi-paned windows, a wide, overhanging, pantiled, hipped roof, and, in the roof, tiny round-topped dormers. The main roof is dominated by a tall clock and ventilator turret. In some ways, the Cochrane Hall, Alva (1929) is the culmination of ideas from all Kerr's Arts and Crafts-styled buildings. It is the Rosemary tiled roof that is most dominant, the steep pitch answering the rising slopes of the Ochil hills behind. At each corner, the roof flows into a hipped wing, connected by porticos to the arched, projecting porch which rises into a curved Dutch gable. The view of the west gable, when approaching Alva from Stirling, is one of the most impressive sights in the Hillfoots. The immense window predominates, inset between north and south wings, and flanked by curved, skewed screen-walls with urn finials.

The former administrative headquarters of the Alloa Cooperative Society (until recently the District Library), dated 1931, was designed by Kerr. It is an excellent example of Thirties classicism, in red Dumfriesshire sandstone, fronting a large vaulted hall onto Mar Street.

Park Primary School (1935), designed by the Melvin office when Kerr was in his late sixties, was innovative for its time. Kerr had designed fairly traditional schools (St John's Primary School (1902), Linwood School (pre-1912) and Houston School (1911–12), Renfrewshire), but Park School uses different design tactics. It is typically Kerr, with dressed stone to the main frontage, grey harled brickwork, and red-tiled hipped roofs. The plan consists of a symmetrical, formal west frontage, out of which come two long,

twenty-four bay, south-facing classroom wings, forming an open court between them. Each immense, thirty-pane window is separated from its neighbour by a narrow buttress. Such use of glass must have been awe-inspiring to pupils accustomed to dark, high-ceilinged Victorian classrooms.

Between 1935 and 1938, Kerr built new showroom and office accommodation (Figures 7.4 and 7.5) for the Alloa Town Council Gas Undertaking. For the showroom frontage, to Bank Street, he produced a plain stone classical elevation, decorated with horizontal balcony railings, the Burgh Arms in relief, and panels decorated with horizontal lines and chevrons, above doors and windows. The remainder is a much more adventurous composition, with vast walls of cream-painted harling punctured by long bands of louvred windows. The rear elevation, to Coalgate, consists of a similarly dominating elevation above three tiny shops, and flanked by twin ovoid towers.

Kerr was over seventy when the Gas Showrooms were completed, and his aspirations to design in the modern vein (and indeed his success) amused young avant-garde architects such as Alan Reiach, a contemporary of his architect son Bryce. His 1936 extension to his Kilncraigs office block, for Paton's Mill, has been reckoned to be the best building of its type and date in Scotland; a white, horizontal, well-proportioned block enclosed within two vertically-proportioned sections, yet continuing the scale and proportion of the 1904 block.

The Pines, Dollar (1938), is a fitting building with which to end. Designed in conjunction with a young assistant, Patrick McNeil, for the latter's parents, it is an interesting combination of Scots vernacular and modernism, in white-painted harling and with a simple slate roof. To the north there are twin gables, one with an iron-framed Venetian bedroom window, and a circular stair tower, and an elegant, stone, carved entrance doorway. To the south is a strip of horizontal, multi-paned upper windows, between the eaves and a string course, and two projecting, lean-to bay windows, reminiscent of Mackintosh's Hillhouse.

Kerr adopted Alloa as his place of work, but he never lived there. For a number of years, he remained faithful to his native Houston, travelling daily by train and reputedly arriving with sketches drawn on his old-fashioned stiff cuffs. He latterly lived at Comely Bank, Edinburgh, where he died in September 1940, still working from his sickbed on proposals for a new school at Tillicoultry.

7.4 and 7.5. Alloa Town Council Gas Undertaking, Bank Street and Coalgate, Alloa, 1934–8. Kerr's 1930s scheme involved a superb classical frontage with a powerful horizontal emphasis and a tall cinemaesque harled rear elevation. This building amused and impressed the young avant-garde architects of the day. (*Top*: RCAHMS; *bottom*: Adam Swan)

This chapter is based on a paper delivered by Adam Swan at the conference 'Mackintosh and his Successful Contemporaries'.

City of Dundee District Council

REFERENCES

I became particularly interested in the work of William Kerr in 1986 when researching the RIAS 'Clackmannan' guide. I had previously been confused by the presence of the unrelated George A. Kerr, who was designing good Art Nouveau-style buildings from the same street in Alloa, at roughly the same time.

This chapter is therefore based on research notes for the RIAS guide, and supplemented by further research for an article for the Charles Rennie Mackintosh Newsletter, Summer 1988, and for the AHSS Strathclyde Group Conference in November 1990.

The main sources of information are as follows:

- Dean of Guild records, Clackmannan District Council.
- Obituaries of William Kerr in the Alloa Advertiser and Alloa Journal, 21 September 1940.
- William Kerr's RIBA membership nomination form, 26 April 1912.
- CRM Society Newsletters nos 43 and 49.
- Article on J.J. Burnet by Dr David Walker in Alastair Service's *Edwardian Architecture and its Origins*, The Architectural Press Ltd, 1975.
- *The Secretary of State's Descriptive Lists of Buildings of Architectural or Historic Interest.* Historic Scotland. Renfrew District and Clackmannan District.
- RIAS Guides to 'The South Clyde Estuary', 1986, by F.A. Walker, and 'Clackmannan and the Ochils', 1987, by Adam Swan.
- Correspondence/discussions with:
  Dr David Walker, Chief Inspector of Historc Buildings, Historic Scotland.
  Miss Elizabeth Kerr, granddaughter.
  Mrs Mary Kerr, daughter-in-law.
  Mrs H Compton, daughter of John Gray.
  Alan MacLean, research student on the work of T.G. Abercrombie.
  Many of the buildings' owners.

The Second Colin McWilliam Memorial Lecture: How Much Should We Respect the Past?

What I have to offer are the views of a bystander on how much, in architecture, we should respect the past. This question *ought* to fall into two parts—how we should treat the buildings which we have already; and how much we should allow them, and the ideas of their makers, to influence the new buildings which we put up now. In fact, as I hope I shall show, those two parts have to be considered together. But why is it necessary to consider the question at all? In many departments of life, respect for the past goes without saying, for example in the law or, for the most part, in religion. In other fields, a respect for the past would seem extraordinary. The reason, I believe, is that, while for centuries the useful and the beautiful could be combined, the machine age has made the technical side of an architect's work more and more *tempting*, giving him and his client the power to astonish and to do too much; so that there is disagreement between architects (as well as between critics and clients) about whether architecture is now primarily a profession like engineering, which cannot be expected to pay much attention to the past, or primarily a long-established art.

Of course, the division between the artist and the technocrat is not a clear division; indeed, strands of each commonly appear, and are needed, in the other. It is a question of emphasis. The contest, started perhaps by William Morris, continued by Gropius, Frank Lloyd Wright, et al., has lasted many rounds, and now, encouraged by the Prince of Wales, the public is joining in, with the effect of a big, friendly dog in a boxing ring—woolly, unwelcome to both contestants, but persistent and likely to affect the outcome. The frame of mind of all those responsible for *new* building crucially affects the future of the buildings which we have already. It is no good toiling to preserve the jewels of the past if they are to be reset in spaghetti; and architects cannot and should not be divided into two separate classes—those who put up new buildings, and those who prop up old ones.

So far as I am concerned, architecture is still an art, if even more complex than it was, and I think that the public will fare better with the artist and his outlook on the past than they will with the technocrat. Artists may lean towards the unfunctional, but technocrats are professionals of all kinds are the more apt, and the more able, to thrust things on the public, to tell them what they *ought* to want.

However, neither artist nor technocrat really cares very much for the opinion of the public. Artists learn from the past, although quite rightly they do not feel bound by an allegiance to it. Copying is not art. Artists struggle towards perfection (which has the great merit, as a goal, of being unattainable). They have to be dissatisfied if they are going to be any good, always discarding and trying to improve upon their latest work. Innovation, as well as skill, is part of art—though not an *essential* part: like craftsmen, artists do not *have* to be original to be good. One wishes some modern architects would think about that.

Moreover artists, of all kinds, are sometimes in advance of their clay-footed contemporaries. They show us things we cannot yet see. They know that some of their predecessors were criticised or ignored, perhaps for years, before they were recognised and applauded. As a result, most artists feel, like the technocrats but for different reasons, that they know better than the public; indeed, which makes it worse, that they actually *ought not* to pander to the public, that they ought to have a free hand, unshackled by the past or by contemporary opinion, and that, if their work is to be judged at all, it should be judged only by other artists or by connoisseurs.

This does not matter with most arts, though we are naturally sorry, and later sometimes ashamed, if as a result the poet or the painter starves. But architecture is too complicated an art for such a pure approach. All arts have their disadvantages. Paintings fade, decay or are destroyed, words lose their meaning—and so forth. Some arts cannot be preserved; some cannot even be recorded, even today. Works of art are like living creatures; they change with age, quickly or slowly, and some live longer than others. The sculptor on the whole comes off best. His work lives longest, changes least and partakes of the universal.

The architect, however, labours under special difficulties. His art is trammelled by practical necessities. I will not mention them all, but, for a start, he cannot afford his own materials. Like any other artist, he is at liberty to conceive what he likes, but in his case someone else must pay to realise it. Thus, if he wishes to practice his art, he is forced to cooperate with people who may not be artists or connoisseurs. Next, his art cannot be hidden. It cannot be stored in a basement, waiting for better times. The public do not have to read books, look at pictures, go to the theatre or listen to music. Architecture, however, is the one art which the public cannot avoid.

The public are already protected by law against many things which, through their representatives in Parliament, they have decided are undesirable. For example, the architect and his or her client are not allowed to pose naked in the street, let alone continuously. It is no good their saying that their pose is very witty, that it makes subtle and interesting historical references, that we must get away from the stuffy old past, when everyone wore clothes all the time, and that if the public cannot appreciate all this then they should shut up about it; nor can the architect and client make a loud noise in a public place (except with an aeroplane which, quite scandalously, is exempted from the law of nuisance); nor can they make offensive statements. They can do all this in private, for example in some nobleman's well-screened park, but not in public. I am not suggesting that those who put up unpopular buildings should be charged with disorderly conduct—or indeed with the offence of 'causing disgust'—but I do believe that the architect and his client have an increasing duty to the public, if only a negative one: they must not give the public what it does not want. Gone are the days when a building was a matter between architect and client only, however enlightened. I believe that failure by most of the artistic establishment to *acknowledge* this difference between architecture and the other arts is one of the things which has got us into trouble, both in the treatment of old buildings and in the design of new ones.

A current illustration of this is provided by the proposed redevelopment of a large office site at Paternoster Square, next to St Paul's Cathedral in London. All the plans were exhibited in a building on the site. The Gallup people took an opinion poll of over a thousand visitors to this exhibition. More than ten per cent of the visitors were architects. Asked how they viewed the proposed development, fourty-seven percent of the public replied 'very favourably'; but forty percent of architects said 'not at all favourably'. Forty-seven per cent of the public thought it would be 'attractive architecturally', compared with only fifteen per cent of the architects.

So the architect, unlike other artists, is immediately brought up against other people, whether he likes or not; and he owes it to Society, I am afraid, to compromise his inclinations and pay attention to the public, allowing them a voice (not just through the Royal Fine Art Commissions) and occasionally a veto. However, he need not compromise his *art*. Indeed, to my mind, an architect is to be most admired when he succeeds in spite of constraints, be they of tradition, bureaucracy, opinion or of site. All Wren's greatest works were compromises, many of them compromises with Royal opinion. Constraints bring out the best in some architects. When Wyatt, at Heveningham Hall in Suffolk, fitted an interior into a half-completed house by Sir Robert Taylor, he produced a greater work of art than in many of the houses he designed from scratch. Surmounting difficulties is part of art. Moreover, all art was originally social, not personal, and architects ought to keep it that way, even if other kinds of artists do not.

But what is it that the public actually want? Do *they* mind about the past at all? Indeed they do, in several different ways. First of all, they mind about *their own* past, the recent past, the past of the living. Most people feel at ease with the familiar and draw strength from it. They will accept change, indeed welcome it in some fields, such as medicine, but they do not relish *a high rate of change*, especially in their surroundings. Too much change is an assault on our feelings and makes us insecure. Today, change of all kinds has speeded up. People do not want to revisit the place of thir birth and find it unrecognisable.

Liking for the past and dislike of change has varied in degree from time to time. The ancient Egyptians clearly found change actually shocking. Their architecture hardly altered for 4,000 years, and when one Pharaoh, Akhnaten, introduced a less formal art, his people, as soon as he was dead, reverted to their previous style and tried to destroy all trace of his existence. They knew about iron, but only used it for toys and charms—many such objects made of iron were found in the wrappings of Tutankhamun's mummy. They must have been wonderful organisers, and at first very inventive, and we must admire them for their pursuit of technical perfection; but I fear that their extreme dislike of change must have made them very boring people.

There have been self-confident periods between then and now when little attention was paid to the past. Today we are, some would say, perhaps over-attached to it again, particularly to the *recent* past, far more so than most of our forebears. The past seems to have got a lot closer. There are too many new museums, too many of them offering entertainment rather than education or scholarship; and some of the confections of the heritage industry, with wax figures in fancy dress set in reconstructions of buildings and streets, sometimes with period smells, are actually a form of *dis*education, a destruction of the past, impressing misleading images on people's minds instead of allowing them to study the genuine and to work things out for themselves. Public acceptance of such things comes from a loss of confidence and is a form of escapism; people look to any sort of past for reassurance because the present seems to them so flawed; and when the future does arrive, we nearly always dislike it. We have come to feel that all changes are for the worse, even changes for the better.

So, to regain public confidence in architecture and in planning, we must moderate the pace of change in our surroundings, even if that means foregoing some apparent benefit. In terms of style, there would be an advantage: all styles are improved by being persisted with, and time allows for experience to be transmitted. Of course, architecture may, indeed should, sometimes take a leap forward—or at any rate a leap—but it must not take leaps all the time. That is trying the public too hard. People, for their peace of mind, should be able to relate most new buildings to their predecessors. It is a reasonable rate of change which has everywhere made the streets of old towns attractive. Rapid change injures atmosphere. Even undistinguished buildings should sometimes be preserved, and open land developed slowly.

This is the only reason for accepting the present craze for 'facadism'—that is to say for shoring up the front of an old building, so that it stands there like a card on edge, then demolishing the rest of it, and replacing that by something entirely modern. In the past, to put an Adam drawing room into a house perhaps 200 years older could turn out very well, but today we overdo it. The effect for those who use the building is that of some films, in which, for example, the camera shows you the great front of Castle Howard and walks you up to the door; you enter and find yourself inside a studio at Shepperton. Sometimes the deception is shown up after dark, when the interior lighting, seen from outside, reveals that the inside of the building bears little relation to its elevation. 'Facadism', besides its insincerity, can also be wastefully expensive. Nevertheless, more people see a building than use it; so 'facadism' can be acceptable, just, if it masks the pace of change.

A particular form of 'facadism' is thrust on the public by planning officers, at least in England, where there are very large numbers of redundant agricultural barns. They are nearly always handsome buildings and, if they are to survive, new uses must be found for them—although some planning officers think that they can refuse *any* new use and at the same time force owners to pay for their repair. When a change of use, say to use as a dwelling, *is* allowed, which happens increasingly seldom, the owner is made to pretend that the building is still a barn; he must have a stove pipe instead of a chimney breast, and skylights instead of windows. It is as if he were hiding in there. You enter the barn expecting to find tractors and straw, but instead you find a smartly attired housewife in a dream kitchen. I believe that this make-believe is unfortunate. Barns and steadings, and indeed all other buildings put up for a special purpose, must, when their purpose vanishes, of course be preserved unaltered if they are pre-eminent examples of their type, but the great majority should be treated not as stage scenery but as useful structures, to be put to new uses honestly. Does this principle apply to redundant churches? They seem to me a special case. It does not seem right to put kitchens, bathrooms, fires and sofas within walls which have absorbed so many emotions. We must try to preserve them in other ways, at least until time has diminished their atmosphere.

Another heresy which afflicts old buildings increasingly is caused by the growth in numbers of archaeologists. Architects are artists; we must cling to that. Good buildings are works of art; they are not archaeological sites, at least until they are ruins, and not always even then. If some Scottish laird of former days, dissatisfied with his portrait by Raeburn, got his artistic wife to add his dog to the picture, their descendant is free to remove the dog. Of course, if the dog had been added by Stubbs or Sir Francis Grant, one would hesitate. If there is a baby in the picture, a later laird is free to paint it out, if he dislikes babies, as one of my uncles did. English Heritage, however, will seldom nowadays allow one to remove inferior additions to a fine building, or to make alterations to it. 'Conserve as found' is the motto, as if History were over. Buildings are increasingly to be treated as documents, to be preserved for study, not as visual objects at all, and not for use. 'Buildings are documents in stone', as Adolf Hitler said.

This attitude is understandable after the dreadful architectural losses which these islands continue to suffer. No is always a safer answer than Yes, and the job of administering controls is always likely to attract rather uncreative people, negative rather than positive. However, I do feel that we must have at least *some* self-confidence. Alterations can at least be recorded. The Landmark Trust does the minimum amount of work to its buildings. We do not like them in what Queen Victoria called 'a very high state of preservation'; and we do not go in for 'conjectural' restoration. If some element of a building is missing altogether, we only provide a modern replacement when it is quite certain what it was like originally, *and* if the building would look ridiculous without it. On the other hand, we do believe that, sometimes, later additions may be removed and later changes reversed. Alterations made to a building are part of it history, and so there should be a presumption in favour of keeping them—unless the original design is of much higher quality than later and perhaps dilapidated work which mars it. In addition, we should not (and we cannot afford to) preserve buildings as dead objects. They are to be occupied by human beings who work in them or cook and wash and who use the rooms. The fact that the architect produces works of art which have to be used, and perhaps later adapted, is just one of the hazards of his kind of art. Occasionally, therefore, it is surely reasonable to make with care some fresh alteration to an old building—and by so doing to add further to its history. Fewer people will be willing to own listed buildings at all if they are to be subjected to a bullying, academic control. Even *if* the archaeological and documentary approach is the correct one, here is surely a case of the best being the enemy of the good.

Some people are tempted to slow the pace of change by *copying* the styles of the past, and sometimes it may be doubly tempting to do that in order to avoid damage to the setting of neighbouring buildings. Architects, unlike other artists, have to cope with the problem of juxtaposition. But it is impossible to recreate the past in architecture, or in anything else, because it is impossible to recreate the outlook on life which went with it. The past is irrecoverable. It is better to accept innovation, of a kind which, though derived from the past, cannot be dismissed as derivative. Lutyens and Soane managed that—indeed Soane derived the flush door in a most original manner. This does not, however, excuse the 'post-modern' style, which is coarse and crude without the saving grace of ignorance. It is also a patronising style. It is as if the architect has said 'So you want a pediment? Well, here is one which is good enough for you.'

As well as caring about their own past, the past of their own place, most people also care about the past of their *country*. They may know very little about it, and some of what they do know may be wrong, but they have absorbed it unconsciously, each day, all their lives, through their skins. History is part of the environment. They have also absorbed their country's customs and conventions, its light and its weather. For this reason, I am afraid, the architect, for new buildings or for old, must always be a native. He must share the past of those who live with his work. In that way, he will get half of it right by instinct. Foreign *influence* is fine, but that influence must be filtered through a native. No foreigner, however assiduous and talented, and however long he tries, can do without that experience. He cannot shake off his own past, nor acquire another. This was unimportant when very few architects worked abroad, and when less attention was paid to the man in the street—indeed, foreign conquerors commonly employed foreign architects; and it is true that foreign architects have brought off great successes, such as Charles Cameron and others in Russia, or indeed James Gibbs in England. Gibbs, incidentally, was a master of *scale*: all his buildings, however grand, are on a human, satisfying scale, and in scale with their setting–considerations which are sometimes neglected nowadays.

I am sorry if I offend any non-Scottish architect, or any Scottish architect who practises abroad; but, to buttress my point, consider *this* country. Nothing can match the bleak elevations of this northern land, often more wall than window, inspired by education, climate and austerity. Good architecture needs a subconscious. When Scottish architects came to embellish and extend the cities of Edinburgh and Glasgow, instinctively they allowed themselves to be influenced by the Greeks. The Greeks were the Scots of the ancient world–not as rich, as complicated or as luxury-loving as their neighbours, but wielding an influence in space and in time out of all proportion to their population. England has nothing like Alexander Thomson. C.R. Mackintosh, inventor of the square hole, was strongly influenced by the architecture of other countries. The result is so original that, once you have studied his work, your eye for architecture and design is permanently altered. Yet no-one looking at the Glasgow School of Art could doubt that it was designed by a Scotsman. Look also at his watercolour drawings of gorse. It is impossible to imagine that foreign architects could have achieved such things by thinking carefully about them.

Some countries are short of good architects. It is tempting for them to invite foreigners to design their buildings, and tempting for foreigners to accept. But it is better for all of us, wherever we are, if each country has buildings with which the natives feel at home, rather than for the whole world to drift towards an international style which is not rooted anywhere. It is just as important to keep national, even regional, feeling in architecture, however faint, as it is to keep using separate languages. We do not want every building to be a departure lounge, despatching us to somewhere else. I would sooner have a single currency than a single architecture.

The past also has a lesson for the present in the use of *materials*. In the distant past, the whole of a building was made of one single material, usually stone, sometimes wood, which of course makes for a fine simplicity and unity. The Greeks used two materials, sometimes three. Today, in the prevailing spirit of disintegration, we use very many, by which I think architecture loses something. Indeed, we are not yet sure of the behaviour of some of these new, processed or composite materials; though one or two, such as asbestos or high-alumina cement, have thrust themselves on our attention. Moreover, in the past, and in some places until very recently, all building materials were local, or at least obtained from the same source. This gives unity to an entire place–a unity of which today one only gets a fleeting glimpse when all the roofs are covered with snow. It also gives continuity to the history of a place. Furthermore, until recently, building materials were hand-made or hand-worked, not machine-made. They were only as accurate as hand and eye can make them, which I am sure renders them more aggreeable to the beholder. Of course, expense, or the size of the building, today nearly always means that the use of such materials is out of the question and one cannot, and should not, keep things going by artificial respiration; but it is an ideal to be aimed at.

In the past, also, buildings were regarded as permanent. Today we know they are not, if only because they are less adaptable than once they were. Consequently, although it is a non-visual consideration, perhaps even a counter-visual one, I do not think that permanent materials, such as granite, marble or slate, however wonderful their texture, should be used in a building whose life is unlikely to be long. It seems as offensively wasteful as a walnut dashboard in a modern car. Buildings designed to last longer than in fact they do are also very un-Green because of the massive amounts of energy used up and wasted in their construction; the kind of buildings which have become consumer durables should be designed as such. Worst of all is when the noble materials of the past are draped over a steel or concrete frame—granite veneer, bricks laid on end, apparently unsupported, and so forth—though that is a pot long since stirred by Walter Gropius and his successors. If the materials do outlive the building, they should be reused, as they have been throughout most of history. It is common in timber-framed houses to find beams with mortises on all four faces, showing that they have been used three times before. The least we can do today is to design buildings with a thought for their realistic length of life, and for their being eventually recycled, as they were in the past.

Architecture is thus not entirely a visual art. In fact, few people except sightseers look carefully at buildings. When they are out-of-doors, they are usually on their way somewhere. What people look at most is the ground. If you want to hide something out-of-doors, such as your tools where you have been working, you should hide them above eye level. People may look at a building which is new to them, once or twice; but from then on, unless they are lovers of architecture, they *feel* it instead. They feel the scale of the building and of its setting, and how it relates to its neighbours. Without looking at it again, they feel how the light and shade are affected by the building and by the elements of its design, be they medieval, classical or modern. Above all, people feel the spaces between buildings, the spaces which buildings create. For the man in the street, if he has no reason to go inside them, the buildings are just the very expensive material which forms the spaces which he feels; and the man in the street is right. His reaction is a correct reaction. Architecture is really about contained spaces, about voids.

In the past, architects, often with great ingenuity, have created modified or preserved marvellous outdoor spaces, but latterly this aspect of their art has fallen victim to that spirit of disintegration and restlessness, which is the spirit of our time. Television documentaries, for example, flit about within their subject, as if viewers had no attention span at all. A recent example of the disintegrationist style is the extension to the National Gallery in London. One feels that the people in charge took a very great deal of trouble, and engaged an excellent builder, but got into difficulties through not employing an architect. Perhaps this is what we are meant to feel. Indeed, the building pokes fun at architecture.

The effect of this spirit on outdoor spaces is that new buildings, each making an individual statement, sometimes a violent one, seem often to be placed on purpose without relationship to each other—indeed sensibly so from their own point of view, since a statement needs a lot of room. The public are good sports; they quite like a vigorous personality, but not too many of them. You cannot have a row of statements; it would look like a platoon of field marshals. Add roads and traffic, which are the enemies of the human scale, and the onlooker is made to feel that the space is formless and infinite, so that there is no point in his starting to walk as he will not get anywhere. A prime example of this is Terminal 4 at Heathrow Airport: I have been there many times, but I still cannot work out where it actually is in relation to anything else.

A well-conceived space, free of clutter, better still a series of spaces, be they streets, squares, courts, closes or wynds, held in by buildings, is a wonderful thing to pass through, even, or perhaps specially, in a poor light or at night, when you cannot examine the detail even if you want to. When considering the demolition of old buildings, however mean, thought should be given to the effect on the spaces which, even by chance, they created.

Another component of architecture which people feel rather than notice, particularly with old buildings, is the ground level, the level of their feet and the level of their eye. Over the years, ground levels change markedly. The ground outside an old building rises; rubbish will have been thrown out in more carefree days, manure added to soil, paths and roads resurfaced many times. The Landmark Trust has found that restoring to its correct level, as exactly as possible, the ground round an old building is almost as important, and as much of an improvement, as restoring the building itself; and, inside, the level of floors and ceilings, and of the sills and heads of windows, have a dramatic effect upon how the occupants feel.

However, although architecture is not a visual art only, there are some non-visual influences which should be kept out of it. It is very tempting, indeed natural, for artists to make their work *didactic*. Writers particularly, painters also, do it often. But the architect's work is thrust on everybody, usually for a long time. Any elements in his design which are not visual should be intelligible and acceptable to most people, and not too transient. Thus, in his design for the new town hall, he may emphasise the splendour of local government, but he should not go in for humour, politics, philosophy or social engineering. Of course, all that is tempting precisely because the public cannot avoid it. Le Corbusier was a dreadful offender here, only really acceptable when designing country churches. Since the late nineteenth century, architecture has been swayed by non-visual theories—modernism, futurism, constructivism, totalitarianism—but architecture should no longer boss people about, or preach. Keep 'isms' out of architecture.

Again, the architect may derive his style from the past, best of all from the past of the place in which he is working, but he should not design a building to be reminiscent of the actual building which it replaces. There are examples of this which look ugly to us because we never saw what was there before. Nor should it be necessary to possess a knowledge of architecture in order to appreciate a building. A good building, old or new, satisfies everybody, at all levels of knowledge and intelligence, from those who just say 'I like it here' to those who study it carefully.

So there it is: humour the public, for whom the past is a vital human need, and who *feel* buildings, and the spaces between them, more than they look at them; and please slow down the pace of change. With all these precepts ever before them, long may the architects of Scotland practise their art, encouraged and surrounded by the friendly ghosts of the past.

Book Reviews

R.J. van Pelt and C.W. Westfall, *Architectural Principles in the Age of Historicism*, Yale University Press, 1991, Hardback, £35,
ISBN 0-300-04999-4.

The title of this book refers to Rudolf Wittkower's work *Architectural Principles in the Age of Humanism* (1947). While Wittkower's classic study addressed the principles which guided architectural thought and practice during the Renaissance, this book attempts to question the relationship between architectural history and contemporary practice through appraising the present in terms of its situation within the Age of Historicism.

The Age of Historicism is defined as 'the epoch when people operate(d) on the assumption "that human affairs can be adequately understood 'historically', that is, by tracing them to their origins and describing their relationship to a process of development through time"' (p. 2). Both authors concur about the problems of relativism and historicism in the study of the history of architecture, which make it difficult to extrapolate principles from the past to guide present practice. So far so good.

This is a 'wordy' book consisting of some 400 pages of text organised into three parts, the central one of which takes the form of a debate. From the initial point of agreement, the arguments diversify in seven chapters, with each author taking an alternate chapter to put forward his viewpoint; the first and final chapters are written by van Pelt.

In his contribution to the debate, Westfall supports the Classical tradition and, in a theoretically-orientated discussion, focuses upon the architecture of political form. Van Pelt develops an argument along the lines of the Judeo-Christian view, which accommodates discussions of both the urban form of ancient Athens and architecture in Germany under the Nazis. Both authors lean heavily on typology to make their arguments.

One of the reasons that the book is so long is that there is a good deal of repetition from chapter to chapter; a penalty, one suspects, of the debate form which the book adopts. Chapters also tend to become rather incoherent by attempting to maintain a balance between didactic summaries and speculative discussions. Included in this, however, are some useful (and readable) summations of certain topics, such as some of the themes of ancient Greek idealising concepts of city and society; and the history of typological thought in architecture (Westfall), spoilt only by the rather cursory dismissal of recent discussion of 'type' (p. 150). By and large, it was the speculative discussions which presented the most difficulties in intelligibility or coherence.

I found this book extremely frustrating to read. At first glance, it looked interesting because of its initial aspirations to deal with the difficult territory of the relation between architectural history and design. However, my experience was that it became, in most parts, almost unreadable to the extent that much was unintelligible. To a large degree, the prose styles of both authors interfered with attempts to understand what was being said; there was a mutual indulgence and indigestible ponderousness of writing styles.

My frustration had increased to such an extent that by the time I encountered Chapter 7 (entitled 'Paradactical Dejection' and one and a half pages in length), I was ready to abandon the rest. The chapter, consisting of a poem by Hölderlin, is followed by van Pelt's footnote withdrawing from the debate and written in what can only be described as purple prose: the final two sentences of the chapter read: 'Therefore it is proper that this bitter allegation will be offered in Chapter Nine, a reckless excursus located in a third part of this book outside the perimeter of the tilting-ground proper. Isolated from the main text I will offer a rendering of the ignoble and spectral puppet show which, standing at the rift, I saw suspended from the Sophoclean stage into the yawning void.'

I could offer further comments on the limited references to original sources and on some annoying spelling mistakes, and point out a few errors such as attributing the Lloyds of London building to Norman Foster (p. 270), but these are extremely minor in comparison to where the main problems seem to lie.

Wittkower's 'Architectural Principles' is brief, profound and readable; this book in my view is none of these. Apart from anything else, the book appears to be orientated to the transatlantic market, and British readers may well find themselves put off by the focus on America, particularly in Westfall's chapters. This alone will, I suspect, make the book less accessible to British students of architecture and architectural practitioners. However, the real limitation is the lack of accessibility to what the authors aspire to say; the initial intention to examine the relation of architectural history to contemporary design is a brave one, but this particular manifestation falls short in form and content.

S. Schafer
University of Edinburgh

Howard Colvin, *Architecture and the After-Life*, Yale University Press, 1991, Hardback, £45, ISBN 0-300-05098-4.

This extensive survey represents something of a new departure for architectural history: it is very much a pioneer study, of exceptional depth and range, in the interaction of the history of architecture and the history of ideas. Similar studies have been attempted for various specific topics and periods, but this book chooses rather to pursue a single idea—the architecture of the commemoration of the dead from prehistory to the nineteenth century—taking an immense number of examples into account. For all the modest disclaimers in the preface that this book is no more than a selection of essays, it gives a very full and complete account of the subject. A survey of this scope would be praiseworthy and interesting in itself, but what gives this book its real claims to innovation is the meticulousness with which Colvin documents the interrelations between periods, giving scrupulous information on the transmission and survival of particular monuments and works of art and their influence on succeeding generations.

Clearly, a full study of a category of building which is so intensely bound up with human ideas and emotions will have to devote unusual attention to tracing the developments of perceptions of the fact and implications of death from society to society, and this Colvin does with considerable success. In doing so, he covers a remarkably wide range: from the prehistoric burials of megalith and tumulus, through a long discussion of the paradigmatic Mausoleum at Halicarnassus and the influence of subsequent attempted reconstructions of it, he progresses to the radical contrasts in sepulchral practice embodied by the classical system of belief which admitted of the apotheosis and deification of the dead as opposed to the first Christian burials around the tombs of the martyrs. Throughout, he is very clear about the ways in which each succeeding phase of commemoration was intended to interact with the spectator and subsequently with posterity, and this clarity carries on into his consideration of chantry chapels and of the social and economic circumstances which led to the construction of the family chapels of Renaissance Italy. The last section of the book begins with the princely burial church in the Catholic south as opposed to the family aisles and chapels of the Protestant north. Aspects of the paganising Enlightenment and the extraordinary latitude allowed to the upper classes by the stratified society of the eighteenth century are considered in relation to the return of the mausoleum, and Colvin's survey ends with the nineteenth-century reversion to the cemetery as the predominant form of burial, closing with the Père Lachaise and the Senatorial tombs in Washington as at least a visual reflection of the Roman sepulchres of the *Via Appia*. The book does not consider any of the more recent trappings of death, some communal memorials, war memorials and crematoria are excluded as essentially belonging to a different strand in the history of ideas from that which is central to the book. It does, however, consider in some detail unbuilt projects, producing illuminating surprises in this area as in many others: for example in the unrealised project for a distinctly Continental and emblematic family aisle in Alloa Kirk projected in exile by the Jacobite Earl of Mar.

As the book is convincing in design, so it abounds with details drawn from little-studied periods and traditions which continually illuminate the main arguments. To choose examples almost at random. Colvin distinguishes in the early modern period, with the greatest precision, the different implications of social structure and shades of religious belief which formed three distinct traditions of sepulture in Scotland, Sweden and England. He does not stop at a very full analysis of the radically different building-types which these variations produced, but investigates and sets forth with admirable clarity the degrees of funerary ostentation which each society would allow to the dead of the upper classes (with the more egalitarian Calvinist societies emerging as the most restrictive of posthumous display) and also traces how far religious practice, however ostensibly reformed, admitted of an implied element of prayer for, as well as commemoration of, the dead. The chapter on Swedish funerary chapels, indeed, is a good example of the ways in which Colvin is continually testing the boundaries of what has hitherto been a kind of *canon* of buildings for discussion: quite apart from the incidental enlightenment of now knowing what the funerary chapel in M.R. James's tale of terror *Count Magnus* must have looked like, the introduction into the argument of these modest, elegantly austere family shrines, filled with hatchments but lacking monuments, functions as a continual and illuminating comparison for the ways in which Anglican funerary practice also tacitly allowed the celebration of status and family to displace considerations of beliefs, death and mortality.

Equally fascinating is the prominence which Colvin gives to the burial of Prince Maurice of Nassau in his gardens at Cleves as early as 1679, doctrinally admissible for a member of the Calvinist royal family of the Netherlands, but also a European precedent for garden burial in the manner of the ancients, whether expressive of active atheism or a reflection of a belief that the importance of a family or an individual had transcended religious affiliation or any sense of common humanity in the face of death. The details which Colvin offers about freethinkers and atheists of the eighteenth century and the epicurean *bizarreries* of their obsequies are a good index of the commendable depth of the documentation which he gives for the attitude of each generation towards death, although one of the very few caveats which might be entered against his general argument is that there may be a yet more complex background of upper-class humanism, neo-Classical ancestor-worship, than even Colvin suggests. Be this as it may, Colvin's tracing of the initially unorthodox practice of burial in parks and gardens, to the point where a mausoleum becomes an index of status and social prestige, is full and assured in its choice of examples, compelling a re-examination of even such familiar and admired buildings as the Hawksmoor mausoleum at Castle Howard in the newly-sharpened context which Colvin's argument provides for it.

This part of the book moves onwards to the consideration of imaginary monuments, imaginary death in the adorning of the French *jardin anglais*, to the tomb of Rousseau on the Island of Poplars and to the Arcadian fantasies of the Parc du Monceau.

Colvin has similarly illuminating and thorough arguments to advance for all the areas on which his work touches, but it is clearly impossible to discuss all of them in this context: it is not mean-spiritedness, but rather an index of the encyclopaedic nature of Colvin's work which causes the indication of a few areas where scholars could develop further the work which he has done. While much is said about the desirability in the early Christian period of burial in proximity to the tomb of a martyr, there is little said about shrines or reliquaries, which surely constitute a significant part of the tradition of sepulture. There is little focus on temporary funerary architecture, although Colvin does give two beautifully-chosen examples of royal catafalques, enough to excite one's interest in this area of architecture or decoration where the most ambitious architectural aspirations could be realised in accommodating materials. Little use is made of epitaph or funerary inscription as an index of feelings or intentions towards death or commemoration (it might be suggested, however, that if Colvin *had* included such sources, they would simply have supported the points elegantly deduced by other methods).

Of particular interest to readers of this journal will be the amount of attention which is paid to Scottish architectural history, particularly in the chapter on the return of the mausoleum, which provides a model for the study of Scottish matters in its lucidity, its awareness of European context and its attention to the cultural and religious circumstances unique to Scotland. The extraordinary Skelmorelie aisle at Largs is discussed in some detail, as is the predictably innovatory mausoleum of the remarkable family of the Clerks of Penicuik. There is also detailed attention paid to the Laird's loft and aisle and to the uniquely Scottish development of burial enclosures or lairs in churchyards.

This latter section, Colvin's continual ability to illuminate known buildings by supplying new contexts, and the breadth and seriousness of argument as well as excellent illustration and design are powerful arguments for reading, and, if possible, buying, a book which should prove a forerunner in the development of architectural history.

Peter Davidson
University of Leiden

James Curl, *The Art and Architecture of Freemasonry*, Batsford, 1991, Hardback, £50, ISBN 0-7134-5827-5.

Some years ago, while sitting in the gloom of the dining room at Brodie Castle (National Trust for Scotland), waiting half an hour for a negative to expose, I took some notes on the bizarre ceiling decoration. The date of the decoration has puzzled architectural historians, but I felt I had made a breakthrough when I realised that the room and the plantation visible through the two windows on the south-west wall were related and that this relationship could best be seen from a point near the centre of the room. This seemed to be confirmed by the discovery that the portrait roundel, of a lady, in the north corner, appeared more handsome from this viewpoint than when viewed from directly below.

I came to no firm conclusions about the room until I received a copy of James Curl's superbly illustrated book for review. To discover that the layout of the room and grounds at Brodie correspond exactly to the 'Layout of a Masonic Lodge', published in 1763, came like a flash of illumination. Had this diagram been published before 1763, I wondered and what did it say about the part traditionally played by Mary Sleigh, wife of Alexander, nineteenth Brodie of that ilk (1697–1754), in laying out the grounds of the estate and in particular the 'wine-goblet' plantation, visible from the centre of the dining room?

This is a book of ideas, and they come thick and fast—almost too fast on occasion, with a tendency to an internal logic, ideas simply based on earlier ideas. But because of those ideas, buildings like Thomas Hamilton's Royal High School (1824–9), with its labyrinthine approach from Regent Terrace, will never be seen in quite the same way again. Equally, his Burns Monument at Alloway (1816–18), perhaps not so surprisingly, becomes a virtuoso piece of masonic as well as Greek revival architecture.

Curl's 'Introductory Study', with sections on the history of the masonic movement, Mozart and Freemasonry, Scottish sundials etc., has removed many of the layers of myth and humbug from an exciting subject which deserves a great deal more study.

For example, the place of women in the masonic tradition needs to be explored further, and the section on Scottish sundials could be given a more critical examination. Much work is also needed on the effects of Freemasonry on modern art and architecture; indeed, an exploration of the art and gardening of Ian Hamilton Finlay could produce another book.

This study is a starting point for much new work, and it is the ideas expressed here which will inspire further reading and research among both architectural historians and general readers, for this is a very readable volume.

Joe Rock
University of Edinburgh

Sam McKinstry, *Rowand Anderson 'The Premier Architect of Scotland'*,
Edinburgh University Press, 1991, Hardback, £35, ISBN 0 7486 0252 6.

In his preface, the author acknowledges the difficulty of deciding between two different methods of writing an architectural monograph: 'the thematic approach forces the writer to analyse, whereas the chronological approach makes him the slave of description'. It is perhaps a pity that in spite of this acknowledgement, he opts for the latter approach, and as a result does indeed become the slave of description, giving almost as much attention to trivial information and the vast bulk of Anderson's more ordinary output as to the major commissions which establish him as a High Victorian architect of the first order, fit to take his place alongside (though not above) the cast of contemporary talents which included, in Scotland, James Matthews, F.T. Pilkington, William Leiper and John James Burnet, and south of the Border G.G. Scott, Burges, Blomfield, Pearson and Bodley.

The author is prey also to the understandable tendency of absorbing wholeheartedly the ideas of his subject, leading him into unfortunate prejudices. There is, for example, a subtext of condescension towards the work of Burn and Bryce, due presumably to Anderson's own criticisms of those instigators of the first Scottish national revival.

Anderson (1834–1921) was to lead the second national revival, based, in the true spirit of the High Victorian era, on the literal adaptation of archaeologically correct detail. It is, of course, a matter of taste whether one prefers the first Burn/Bryce revival, based on functional planning combined with picturesque massing and lively skylines, with detail extracted from the fifteenth and sixteenth centuries, or the second revival, also based on functional planning, but with a more restricted, 'correct' exterior expression, based, for domestic work, on seventeenth century, and, for churches, on anything medieval and Scottish. The danger of the second sort of approach in Scotland for churches, of course, is the relatively limited fund of surviving examples of medieval Gothic or Romanesque from which to quote. This is revealingly demonstrated in Anderson's oeuvre in his determination to build onto every one of his nineteenth-century churches a circa 1000 Brechin round tower (executed only once, at Dunfermline).

The two different approaches are expressed in two dimensions by, on the one hand, Billings's romantically sketchy illustrations for *The Baronial and Ecclesiastical Antiquities of Scotland* (1845–52), and on the other by the precise linear drawings of the National Art Survey (from 1893) whose inception and eventual publication (1921) is due entirely to Anderson.

The book also contains unexplained condemnations of some of Anderson's predecessors and contemporaries: John Henderson of Edinburgh, who preceded Anderson as architect to the Episcopal Church, was, apparently, 'not a great architect'; John Dick Peddie is 'the largely uninspired Peddie'. Sweeping statements of this sort are difficult to swallow, and unnecessary. The author's authority on Rowand Anderson is not in question, but generalities of this sort should be avoided until such time as the largely unexplored (largely unpublished) but exciting area of nineteenth-century Scottish architecture has been more thoroughly elucidated.

The impression given in the book of much of Anderson's executed work leads this reader to the conclusion that the second revival was successful only later in the century, in the hands of Anderson's disciples (former assistants and pupils, all of whom are very helpfully gathered together in the second appendix), a galaxy of talents, including A.G. Sydney Mitchell, George Washington Browne and R.S. Lorimer, and in the hands of others who were directly influenced by his ideas, including A.N. Paterson and C.R. MacKintosh; all of whom seem to have been able to use traditional Scottish forms in a new and inventive way.

But this impression—which leaves Anderson with the role of instigator of ideas and educator, rather than designer of note—is probably misleading, and the book is partly to blame for the injustice, being visually inept. Poor-quality black-and-white photographs give not even the slightest indication of important interior and exterior works, executed—for the first time by a Scottish architect—with the full polychrome palette of Street, Butterfield and Burges. The splendours of the interiors of Mount Stuart, the National Portrait Gallery (Figure 1), St Cuthbert's Episcopal Church, Colinton, Bellevue Catholic Apostolic Church and Edinburgh University's McEwan Hall cannot be guessed at. In the text, we hear of Anderson designing the first Byzantine revival church in Scotland—in polychrome—at Galston (Kilmarnock and Loudon), decorating his churches with stencilling, distemper and murals by Phoebe Traquair and William Hole, and going to the lengths of oiling the red masonry columns of St Andrew's Episcopal Church, St Andrews, to enhance their colour. He was the favoured architect of the third Marquess of Bute, a keen revivalist and architectural patron, himself a colourful character who had employed William Burges, and who 'would frequent these surroundings [Burges's Cardiff Castle and Castle Coch] gorgeously clad in the robes of medieval saints'.

The book also attests to Anderson's enormous importance as campaigner for an improved, craft-based, architectural education, and for improved status for the profession within the RSA. His status is reflected in his having been president of the architecture section of the National Association for the Advancement of Art and Its Application to Industry (1889), while William Morris presided over the Applied Arts. He was founding member and first president of the IAS (RIAS from 1916), and the first home-based Scotsman to receive the RIBA Gold Medal.

None of this tallies with the humdrum presentation of this rather grey book. This is an important work, the result of wide-ranging researches by the author, who commits to paper for the first time many important facts about Sir Rowand Anderson, but also about the world in which he worked. It is a pity that the RIAS and Scottish Arts Council were not able to celebrate the 150th Jubilee of the foundation of the IAS in 1990, in this

1. Sir Robert Rowand Anderson, National Portrait Gallery, 1884–9. Central hall from gallery, with capitals sculpted by students of Edinburgh College of Art (1897) and painted arcade frieze by William Hole, 1887–1901. (© Antonia Reeve Photography, for the National Galleries of Scotland)

very necessary work on a nationally important Victorian architect, with a book of slightly more inspiring appearance.

Gillian Haggart
Historic Scotland

The Architectural Heritage Society
of Scotland Appeal

Benefactors
The Charities Aid Foundation, with
    Enterprise Oil Company Ltd
The Esmee Fairbairn Charitable Trust

Supporters
The Dunard Fund
J.R. Stuart Esq
The Russell Trust
Donald Ian Findlay MA FSA FSA (Scot)
Dorothy Joan Shand
The William Adam Trust
The Hon. Sir Steven Runciman, CH

Donors
Jane A. Kellett
Lady Robertson
William Rodger Esq
Miss M.M. Roddan
Ronald and Jane Duff
Kyle and Carrick Civic Society
The Lesley David Trust

Contributors
Mrs Sheila C Arkless
Miss Bridget Blackmore
Mr David M Burns Esq
Campbell and Smith Construction Co.
    Ltd
Clydesdale Bank Plc
H.M. Colvin Esq
Miss Margaret Croft
Colin D. Donald Esq
Alexander Dunbar Esq
L.R.K. Fyffe Esq
Caroline Gould

Hurd Rolland Partnership
Joan M. Low
M.K. Macdonald
Iain MacIvor Esq
N.M. Macnaughton
C. McWilliam
Mrs W.W. Martin
Rosemary Miller
J.R. Morris
The Orcome Trust
Mrs Margaret Richards
John Sanders Esq
Barry E. Sealey Esq
Patrick W. Simpson Eqs
Professor E. Mary Smallwood
Miss Nora E. Smith
Charles W. Stewart Esq
Succoth Charitable Trust
Major M.P. Taitt
Mrs Elizabeth Uldall
Commander S.H. Walker OBE DSC
    RD
R.K. Martin Esq
John Higgitt Esq
Mrs Virginia Holt
John Younger Trust
William D. Prosser
Mrs Marion Fairbairn
R.D. Cramond Esq CBE
P.W. Simpson Esq
Dr D.J.B. Marke
L.A.L. Rolland
Margot Butt
Miss Judith Scott
Elizabeth Strong
Deborah Howard
Colin Thompson Esq
Page and Park Architects
Miss Jean Jack